Conceptual Foundations of Language Science

Series editors
Mark Dingemanse, *Max Planck Institute for Psycholinguistics*
N. J. Enfield, *University of Sydney*

Editorial board
Balthasar Bickel, *University of Zürich*, Claire Bowern, *Yale University*, Elizabeth Couper-Kuhlen, *University of Helsinki*, William Croft, *University of New Mexico*, Rose-Marie Déchaine, *University of British Columbia*, William A. Foley, *University of Sydney* , William F. Hanks, *University of California at Berkeley*, Paul Kockelman, *Yale University*, Keren Rice, *University of Toronto*, Sharon Rose, *University of California at San Diego*, Frederick J. Newmeyer, *University of Washington*, Wendy Sandler, *University of Haifa*, Dan Sperber *Central European University*

No scientific work proceeds without conceptual foundations. In language science, our concepts about language determine our assumptions, direct our attention, and guide our hypotheses and our reasoning. Only with clarity about conceptual foundations can we pose coherent research questions, design critical experiments, and collect crucial data. This series publishes short and accessible books that explore well-defined topics in the conceptual foundations of language science. The series provides a venue for conceptual arguments and explorations that do not require the traditional book-length treatment, yet that demand more space than a typical journal article allows.

In this series:

1. N. J. Enfield. *Natural causes of language*.

Natural causes of language

Frames, biases, and cultural transmission

N. J. Enfield

language science press

N. J. Enfield. 2014. *Natural causes of language: Frames, biases, and cultural transmission* (Conceptual Foundations of Language Science 1). Berlin: Language Science Press.

This title can be downloaded at:
http://langsci-press.org/catalog/book/48
© 2014, N. J. Enfield
Published under the Creative Commons Attribution 4.0 Licence (CC BY 4.0):
http://creativecommons.org/licenses/by/4.0/
ISBN: 978-3-944675-50-3

Cover and concept of design: Ulrike Harbort
Typesetting: Nick Enfield, Sebastian Nordhoff
Proofreading: Timo Buchholz, Stefan Hartmann, Christian Pietsch, Klara Kim, Anelia Stefanova
Fonts: Linux Libertine, Arimo
Typesetting software: X∃LATEX

Language Science Press
Habelschwerdter Allee 45
14195 Berlin, Germany
langsci-press.org

Storage and cataloguing done by FU Berlin

Language Science Press has no responsibility for the persistence or accuracy of URLs for external or third-party Internet websites referred to in this publication, and does not guarantee that any content on such websites is, or will remain, accurate or appropriate. Information regarding prices, travel timetables and other factual information given in this work are correct at the time of first publication but Language Science Press does not guarantee the accuracy of such information thereafter.

In memory of Grant Evans: colleague, mentor, and friend

Contents

Acknowledgements	vii
Preface	ix

1 Causal units — 1
- 1.1 How we represent language change — 3
- 1.2 Linguistic systems — 4
- 1.3 Linguistic items — 6
- 1.4 Thinking causally about language change — 7
- 1.5 The problem with tree diagrams — 8

2 Causal frames — 9
- 2.1 Distinct frames and forces — 10
- 2.2 MOPEDS: A basic-level set of causal frames — 13
  - 2.2.1 Microgenetic (action processing) — 13
  - 2.2.2 Ontogenetic (biography) — 14
  - 2.2.3 Phylogenetic (biological evolution) — 14
  - 2.2.4 Enchronic (social interactional) — 15
  - 2.2.5 Diachronic (social/cultural history) — 15
  - 2.2.6 Synchronic (representation of relations) — 16
- 2.3 Interrelatedness of the frames — 17
- 2.4 The case of Zipf's length-frequency rule — 17

3 Transmission biases — 21
- 3.1 Cultural epidemiology — 22
- 3.2 Biased transmission — 23
- 3.3 Some known biases — 25
- 3.4 A scheme for grounding the biases — 26
  - 3.4.1 Exposure — 28
  - 3.4.2 Representation — 29
  - 3.4.3 Reproduction — 30

		3.4.4	Material	32
		3.4.5	Networks	33
	3.5	Causal anatomy of transmission		35

4 The item/system problem — 37
    4.1 A transmission criterion — 38
    4.2 Defining properties of systems — 39
    4.3 Relations between relations — 40
    4.4 More complex systems — 44
    4.5 Are cultural totalities illusory? — 49

5 The micro/macro solution — 51
    5.1 The combinatoric nature of cultural items in general — 53
    5.2 Solving the item/system problem in language — 55
    5.3 Centripetal and systematizing forces — 56
    5.4 On normal transmission — 56
        5.4.1 Sociometric closure — 58
        5.4.2 Trade-off effects — 59
        5.4.3 Item-utterance fit, aka content-frame fit — 59
    5.5 A solution to the item/system problem? — 60

6 Conclusion — 63
    6.1 Natural causes of language — 64
    6.2 Toward a framework — 64

Bibliography — 67

Index — 78
    Name index — 78
    Subject index — 81

Acknowledgements

In writing this book I have benefited greatly from communication with Balthasar Bickel, Claire Bowern, Rob Boyd, Morten Christiansen, Jeremy Collins, Grev Corbett, Stephen Cowley, Sonia Cristofaro, Bill Croft, Jennifer Culbertson, Dan Dediu, Mark Dingemanse, Daniel Dor, Grant Evans†, Nick Evans, Bill Foley, Bill Hanks, Martin Haspelmath, Larry Hyman, Jennifer Johnson-Hanks, Simon Kirby, Wolfgang Klein, Chris Knight, Paul Kockelman, Michael Lempert, Steve Levinson, Elena Lieven, Hugo Mercier, Pieter Muysken, Csaba Pléh, Joanna Rączaszek-Leonardi, Keren Rice, Peter Richerson, Seán Roberts, Giovanni Rossi, Wendy Sandler, Jack Sidnell, Chris Sinha, Hedvig Skirgård, Kenny Smith, Dan Sperber, Sune Vork Steffensen, Monica Tamariz, Jordan Zlatev, and Chip Zuckerman. I thank participants at the conference *Naturalistic Approaches to Culture* (Balatonvilagos 2011), the conference *Social Origins of Language* (London 2011), the conference *Language, Culture, and Mind V* (Lisbon 2012), the workshop *Rethinking Meaning* (Bologna 2012), the *Minerva-Gentner Symposium on Emergent Languages and Cultural Evolution* (Nijmegen 2013), and the retreat *Dependencies among Systems of Language* (Château de la Poste 2014) for comments, reactions, and inspiration.

For troubleshooting with LaTeX I am grateful to Sebastian Nordhoff and Seán Roberts. This work is supported by the European Research Council (grant 240853 *Human Sociality and Systems of Language Use*, 2010–2014), and the Max Planck Institute for Psycholinguistics, Nijmegen. Chapters 2–5 are thoroughly revised versions of previously published works: as chapters in *Social Origins of Language* (OUP, 2014, edited by D. Dor, C. Knight, and J. Lewis), and *The Cambridge Handbook of Linguistic Anthropology* (CUP, 2014, edited by N. J. Enfield, P. Kockelman, and J. Sidnell). Further, certain parts draw on sections of Enfield (2008, 2013, chap. 11).

I dedicate this book to Grant Evans (1948–2014): historian, sociologist, and anthropologist of Southeast Asia. In our conversations over nearly 20 years, Grant always challenged my natural tendency to focus on items. He never stopped pushing me to acknowledge the causal reality of socio-cultural systems. His intellectual engagement has been one of the main motivations for me to confront the item/system problem that is at the heart of this book.

Preface

This essay explores some conceptual foundations for understanding the natural causes of linguistic systems. At the core of it are three ideas.

The first is that causal processes in linguistic reality apply in multiple frames or "time scales" simultaneously, and we need to understand and address each and all of these frames in our work. This is the topic of Chapter 2.

This leads to the second idea. For language and the rest of culture to exist, its constituent parts must have been successfully diffused and kept in circulation in the social histories of communities. This relies on convergent processes in multiple causal frames, and depends especially on the micro-level behavior of people in social interaction. This is the topic of Chapter 3.

The third idea, building on this, is that the socially-diffusing parts of language and culture are not just floating around, but are firmly integrated within larger systems. We need to understand the link between the parts and the higher-level systems they belong to. This point is underappreciated. Inferences made from facts about *items* are often presented without reflection as being facts about the whole *systems* they fit into. Tree diagrams help to perpetuate this problem. It is difficult to assess work on the history of languages if that work does not offer a solution to the item/system problem. Facts about items need to be linked to facts about systems. We need a causal account of how it is that mobile bits of knowledge and behavior become structured cultural systems such as languages. This is the topic of Chapter 4 (where the problem is articulated) and Chapter 5 (where a solution is offered).

In exploring these ideas, this book suggests a conceptual framework for explaining, in causal terms, what language is like and why it is like that. It does not attempt to explain specifics, for example why one language has verbal agreement involving noun class markers and another language does not. But the basic elements of causal frames and transmission biases, and the item/system dynamics that arise, are argued to be adequate for ultimately answering specific questions like these. Any detailed explanation will work – explicitly or implicitly – in these terms. Here is another thing this book does not do: It does not give detailed or lengthy case studies. Instead, the examples are illustrative, and many

Preface

can be found in the literature referred to. The *Conceptual Foundations of Language Science* book series is intended for short and readable studies that address and provoke conceptual questions. While methods of research on language keep changing, and often provide much-needed drive to a line of work, the underlying conceptual work – always independent from the methods being applied – must provide the foundation.

1 Causal units

What is the causal relationship between the bits of language – sounds, words, idioms – and the whole systems that we call languages? A way into this question is to ask why any two languages might share a trait. There are four possible reasons:

0. *Universal presence*: All languages must have the trait; therefore A and B have it.

1. *Vertical transmission*: The trait was inherited into both A and B from a single common ancestor language.

2. *Horizontal transmission*: The trait was borrowed into one or both of the languages (from A into B, from B into A, or from a third language into both A and B).

3. *Internal development*: The trait was internally innovated by both A and B, independent from each other.[1]

Leaving aside universals, the three possibilities (1–3) involve processes that are often considered to be qualitatively different, namely (1) inheritance (from mother to daughter language), (2) borrowing (from neighbouring language to neighbouring language through contact among speakers), and (3) natural, internally motivated development. But at a fundamental level these processes are not distinct:

> Language change by contact or otherwise is a process of social diffusion. The standard analytical distinction between internal and external linguistic mechanisms diverts attention from the fact that these are instances of the same process: the diffusion of cultural innovation in human populations. (Enfield 2005: 197)

---
[1] If the two languages possessed the same starting conditions for the same internal innovation, the question arises as to why they shared those starting conditions in the first place. This takes us back to the question "Why do two languages share a trait?".

1 Causal units

This is the conclusion I came to when considering possible explanations for convergence of structure among neighboring language communities in the mainland Southeast Asia area. As I put it then:

> Areal linguistics invites us to revise our understanding of the ontology of languages and their historical evolution, showing that the only units one needs to posit as playing a causal role are individual speakers and individual linguistic items. These unit types are mobile or detachable with respect to the populations they inhabit, arguing against essentialism in both linguistic and sociocultural systems.
>
> Areal linguistics presents significant challenges for standard understandings of the ontology of language from both spatial and temporal perspectives. Scholars of language need to work through the implications of the view that "the language" and "the community" are incoherent as units of analysis for causal processes in the historical and areal trajectories of language diffusion and change. (Enfield 2005: 198)

In this book I explore some implications of these conclusions. When we grapple with puzzles of inheritance, contact, and diffusion in the history of languages, we have to confront the item/system problem (see Chapter 4), and its collateral challenges.

The three processes mentioned above – inheritance, borrowing, innovation – can only take place when there is social contact between people, and successful diffusion of types of behavior in communities. These are causal preconditions. For any of the three processes to succeed, several things have to happen. People have to start saying things in new ways (or saying new things), exposing others in their personal network to new ideas. Those who are exposed then have to copy this new behavior, and they have to be motivated to do so. This in turn has to expose more people in their social networks, as well as further exposing those who began the process in the first place, validating and encouraging the new behavior, and leading it to take further hold. At a fundamental level, the three ways that something can get into a language are indistinguishable from one another. If there are differences, they have to do with where the idea came from, how natural the idea is (i.e. how much it makes sense and perhaps how much it helps cut corners in communication or processing), and what is the social identificational value of the idea.

1.1 How we represent language change

One way to understand something is to look at the history of events that created it. Consider the history of any type of life form. The central formative events take place in populations. Individuals inherit characteristics – for example, from the genome of their parents – and when those inherited characteristics can vary between individuals in a population, an individual with one variant might have a better chance of surviving than someone with another variant. When higher likelihood of survival means higher likelihood of reproduction, this can increase the frequency of an advantageous variant in the population. In time, the variant comes to be carried by all individuals. Two or more distinct populations emerge, and these may then be regarded as separate species. While the new populations share a common ancestor, they are now essentially different.

This way of thinking about the causal basis of species in terms of population dynamics is central in the theory of biological evolution (Darwin 1859; Mayr 1970). It can be applied to the evolution of life forms of all kinds, and to cultural types including kinship systems, technologies, and languages (Dawkins 1976; Mesoudi et al. 2006). The process of speciation in any of these forms of life implies relations of common ancestry that may be represented using a tree diagram. Figure 1.1 illustrates.

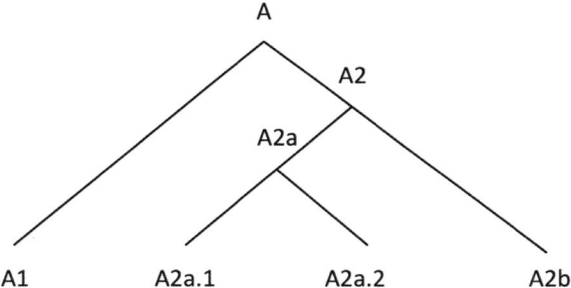

Figure 1.1: Tree diagram representing divergence by descent with modification. A1, A2a.1, A2a.2, and A2b are common descendants of A.

Diversification of languages, as in the history of great stocks like Bantu, Austronesian, and Indo-European, has long been represented with tree diagrams of this kind, in which the ostensible units of analysis are languages. By taking the language as the unit of analysis, tree diagrams must assume that languages cohere as units. Is this a fair assumption? Are language systems coherent, natural kinds? Or do we only imagine them to be?

1 Causal units

When tree diagrams are used to represent the history of diversification within a family of languages, there is an analogy with the kind of evolution seen in life forms that show a total or near-total bias toward vertical transmission in evolution, namely vertebrates such as primates, birds, fish, and reptiles. So let us consider what the tree diagram means in the case of vertebrate natural history. Each binary branching in the tree represents a definitive split in a breeding population. The populations represented by daughter nodes inherit traits that were found in the parent population. Members of the daughter populations also commonly inherit modifications of the parent traits that significantly distinguish the two daughter populations from each other. Inheritance happens in events of sexual reproduction, in which complete genotypes are bestowed in the conception of new individuals. This encapsulation of the genome in causal events of inheritance ensures the vertical transmission that a tree diagram represents so well. In vertebrate species, when two populations are no longer able to interbreed, they can no longer contribute to each other's historical gene pool. This would be *horizontal transmission*, something that is essentially absent from vertebrate evolution (though with some caveats; Koonin 2009). The tree representation is adequate in the case of vertebrate speciation for one reason: the tree diagram does not capture horizontal transmission. The vertebrate genome is essentially acquired by the individual organism as a bundle. So the complete organism can reasonably be treated as a unit for describing transmission and change in phylogeny. The vehicle for replication is the individual organism as defined by the structurally coherent entity that we call the body.

The problem is that while vertebrates have been implicitly taken to be the model for language, they are not like language in causal terms. They are not even representative of life forms in general. Most forms of life, including not only the non-animal Eukaryotes, but also the Bacteria and Archaea, are not subject to strong vertical transmission constraints (Boto 2010). Most forms of life lack the bounded body plans that delineate vehicles or interactors for passing on replicable traits. The overall phenotypic structures of "individuals" in many species are to a large degree emergent. Evolutionary processes can be more clearly seen to operate on *parts* of organisms (Dawkins 1976).

1.2 Linguistic systems

People find it easy to accept "the language" as a unit of causal analysis. Our intuitions suggest that languages are effectively bounded, whole systems. We readily think of them as organisms. But they can also be thought of as focussed bundles of items. Indeed they should be thought of in this way, for the "linguistic system" is not a natural kind.

The point has been made for linguistic systems with most clarity and rigor by Le Page & Tabouret-Keller (1985). A prerequisite to the idea of a language (e.g. English) is the idea of a group of people who speak it. But as Le Page and Tabouret-Keller (1985) put it:

> Groups or communities and the linguistic attributes of such groups have no existential locus other than in the minds of individuals. (p. 4) We do not ourselves then need to put a boundary around any group of speakers and say "These are the speakers of Language A, different from Language B", except to the extent that the people think of themselves in that way, and identify with or distance themselves from others by their behavior. (p. 9)

The point was made a half-century ago for social systems more generally by the anthropologist Edmund Leach (1964), in critiquing the structuralism of Radcliffe-Brown and students (Fortes & Evans-Pritchard 1940):

> Social systems were spoken of as if they were naturally existing real entities and the equilibrium inherent in such systems was intrinsic. (p. x) I do not consider that social systems are a natural reality. In my view, the facts of ethnography and of history can only *appear* to be ordered in a systematic way if we impose upon these facts a figment of thought. (p. xii)

Fair enough. But there must be some natural reality upon which we may impose our figments of thought. One candidate is the economy of *bits* of language or culture, each of which has mobility: the words and other things that we can borrow from outside, without having to borrow the whole systems they come from. As Hudson (1996: 22) puts it:

> We need to distance ourselves somewhat from the concepts represented by the words *language* and *dialect*, which are a reasonable reflection of our lay culture, called "common-sense knowledge", but not helpful in sociolinguistics. First, we need a term for the individual "bits of language" to which some sociolinguistic statements need to refer, where more global statements are not possible.

Hudson introduces *linguistic item* as a term for this unit with causal reality. Suppose that items – in bundles – are what we impose an essence upon when

1 Causal units

we imagine languages. Our vernacular language names would be labels for these imposed, imagined essences.[2]

1.3 Linguistic items

The idea that languages are causally real units gets weaker when we think of the mechanisms of language transmission, both across and within generations. There are two problems for the language-as-real-system idea. The first is that causal processes of transmission can be observed most concretely operating upon items (e.g., in the borrowing and learning of words), not on whole systems. The second is that horizontal transmission occurs. All parts of a language appear in principle to be independently mobile (though of course some bits of language travel more freely than others; Thomason & Kaufman 1988; Curnow 2001; Thomason 2001). Now consider these points more closely.

What is transmitted in language history? It is not the whole system at once, but the components of the system, piece by piece and chunk by chunk, in millions of distinct events. Never all at once but at separate moments, over days, weeks, months and years. To be sure, the result of language transmission is a high degree of overlap among idiolects in a human population.[3] The overlap is so high that our idiolects are practically indistinguishable. And this reassures us that systems are real wholes. How does this degree of idiolect overlap come about?

Part of the answer is that speech communities are inward-focused. People in a group transmit linguistic items when they converse and interact. This creates an economy of signs, in the sense of Zipf (1949). When people in a group interact repeatedly, more signs come to be shared among those people. And the more that signs are shared, the more readily those people interact. This feedback effect in the social circulation of linguistic items is both a result of, and a cause of, common ground in a community. People have more common ground because they interact more; they interact more because they have more common ground. The basic causal units, though, are the shared items, not the systems that emerge.

The second problem with "the language" as a natural unit is the ease of borrowing linguistic items. Languages constantly incorporate new structures, and quickly. When confronted with this kind of horizontal transmission, students of language change have looked for ways to distinguish it from a vertical signal,

---

[2] If the reader is concerned that the true holistic system nature of languages is being underestimated, see Chapter 4, below.

[3] On idiolect overlap or convergence, cf. Bakhtin (1981), Hockett (1987: 106–107, 157–158), Lee (1996: 227–228).

usually to then exclude it. But if horizontal transmission is so widespread, this should cause people to doubt the value of a model in which vertical transmission is the main object of interest for representing and understanding language history. With a proper understanding of the causality of language change, we see that tree diagrams that take "the language" as the unit of analysis not only abstract from reality, they distort it. They are poor conceptual tools for understanding the ontology of language. The solution is to change our assumptions about the causal units involved.

For Darwinian evolution to occur, there must be a population of essentially equivalent but non-identical units. These units must inherit traits from comparable units that existed prior to them. And these inheritable traits must show variation that can result in comparable units having different chances of surviving to pass on those traits to a new generation. What are the units? In the case of vertebrates, a received view is that two sorts of units work together: organisms, and genes. Organisms are vehicles for replicating genes. In vertebrates, the vehicles for inheritance of traits are the bodies of individuals. Each body is a phenotypic instantiation of the system. But here is the problem. The situation with languages is not like this at all.

1.4 Thinking causally about language change

We want a causal account of languages as historically evolved systems. To think concretely about this, consider the following. All the conventional bits of language you learned as an infant were created by enormous chains of social interaction in the history of a population. Each link in the chain was an observable instance of usage, a micro-scale cycle of transmission, going from public (someone uses a structure when speaking) to private (a second person's mental state is affected when the structure is learnt or entrenched) and back to public (the second person uses the structure, exposing someone else), and so on. This may seem to be an overly micro-perspective way of putting it. But it is important to be explicit about the proximal mechanisms of transmission. Causal statements about language often highlight only a part of what is going on.

Consider (1) and (2):

1. *Knowledge of grammar causes instances of speaking.*

2. *Instances of speaking cause knowledge of grammar.*

Statement (1) focuses on competence. It points to mechanisms of, and prerequisites for, saying things. Statement (2) focuses on performance and emphasizes its outcomes. We learn about language from what people say. But there is no contradiction between the statements shown in (1) and (2). They are ways of framing the same thing. Competence and performance are equally indispensable in the processes of historical evolution that determine and constrain what a language can be like. Words are effectively competing for our selection (Croft 2000). If all goes well, we select the items that best enable us to manipulate other people's attentional and interpretive resources (Enfield 2013: 16–17).

1.5 The problem with tree diagrams

Tree diagrams of language diversification are good for some things, but they are not good for representing causal processes of language history, nor the natural, causal ontology of languages and language relatedness. The tree diagram assumes that we are primarily interested in one form of transmission of heritable characteristics, namely, vertical transmission of features from a parent to a daughter language, normally through first language acquisition in children. The alternative – horizontal transmission, i.e., transmission of features between languages whose speakers are in contact, normally involving adult language learning – is acknowledged but is regarded as noise that needs to be factored out from the vertical historical signal of primary interest (cf. Dixon 1997, and note that some recent work applying new methods is showing promising signs of a shift in direction here; e.g., Reesink et al. 2009).

The tree diagram is a methodological simplification. It requires us to abstract from the causal facts. Of course this abstraction may be a harmless practical necessity. But our question is whether the abstraction inherent in the tree diagram does *conceptual* harm. I think the answer is yes. It directs our attention away from the causal mechanisms that define language as an evolutionary process, and languages as evolved systems.

To begin to think causally we first need to explore the multiple frames within which causal processes may be effected. This is the topic of the next chapter.

2 Causal frames

If you really want to understand language, you will have to study a lot of different things. Here are some:

- The finely-timed perceptual, cognitive, and motoric processes involved in producing and comprehending language

- The early lifespan processes by which children learn linguistic and communicative knowledge and skills

- The evolutionary processes that led to the unique emergence of the cognitive capacities for language in our species

- The ways in which the things we say are moves in sequences of social actions

- The mechanisms and products of language change, with links between historical processes and evolutionary processes

- Linguistic variation and its role in how historical change in language takes place in human populations

- Things that can be described without reference to process or causation at all, as seen in linguistic grammars, dictionaries, ethnographies, and typologies, where relationships rather than processes are the focus

These different points of focus correspond roughly with distinct research perspectives. But they do not merely represent disciplinary alternatives. The different perspectives can be seen to fit together as parts of a larger conceptual framework.

To give some outline to that framework, I here define six interconnected frames for orienting our work. They remind us of the perspectives that are always available and potentially relevant, but that we might not be focusing on. They do not constitute a definitive set of frames – there is no definitive set – but they are

2 Causal frames

useful. They correspond well to the most important causal domains. They conveniently group similar or tightly interconnected sets of causal mechanism under single rubrics. And together they cover most of what we need for providing answers to our questions in research on language.

The frames are *Microgenetic, Ontogenetic, Phylogenetic, Enchronic, Diachronic,* and *Synchronic*. The meanings of these terms are explicated below. As a mnemonic, they spell MOPEDS. Frames like these are sometimes referred to as *time scales*. But calling them "scales" is not accurate. It implies that they all measure the same thing, just with arbitrarily different units of measure – seconds versus minutes versus hours, etc. But the difference between, say, ontogenetic and diachronic (ditto for the other frames) is not defined in terms of abstract or objective units of the same underlying stuff – time, in this case. The frames are defined and distinguished in terms of different types of underlying processes and causal-conditional mechanisms. For each frame, what matters most is how it works, not how long it takes.

By offering a scheme of interrelated causal frames as part of a conceptual framework for research on language, I want to stress two points.

The first is that these frames are most useful when we keep them conceptually distinct. Kinds of reasoning that apply within one frame do not necessarily apply in another, and data that are relevant in one frame might not be relevant (in the same ways) in another. Mixing up these frames leads to confusion.

The second point is that for a full understanding of the things we study it is not enough just to understand these things from within all of the different frames. The ideal is also to show how each frame is linked to each other frame, and, ultimately, how together the frames reveal a system of causal forces that define linguistic reality.

2.1 Distinct frames and forces

The ethologist Niko Tinbergen famously emphasized that different kinds of research question may be posed within different theoretical and methodological frames, and may draw on different kinds of data and reasoning (Tinbergen 1963). See Table 2.1.

Tinbergen's four questions were applied in studying the behavior of non human animals. The distinctions were designed to handle communication systems such as the mating behavior of stickleback fish, not the far greater complexities of language, nor the rich cultural contexts of language systems. If we are going to capture the spirit of Tinbergen's idea, we need a scheme that better covers the

2.1 Distinct frames and forces

Table 2.1: Distinct causal/temporal frames for studying animal behavior, after Tinbergen (1963).

Causal	What is the mechanism by which the behavior occurs?
Functional	What is the survival or fitness value of the behavior?
Phylogenetic	How did the behavior emerge in the course of evolution?
Ontogenetic	How does the behavior emerge in an individual's lifetime?

phenomena specific to language and its relation to human diversity.

Many researchers of language and culture have emphasized the need to monitor and distinguish different causal frames that determine our perspective. These include researchers of last century (Saussure 1916; Vygotsky 1962) through to many of today (Tomasello 2003; MacWhinney 2005; Rączaszek-Leonardi 2010; Cole 2007; Donald 2007; Larsen-Freeman & Cameron 2008; Uryu et al. 2014; Lemke 2000, 2002). We now consider some of the distinctions they have offered.

The classical two-way distinction made by Saussure (1916) – *synchronic* versus *diachronic* – is the tip of the iceberg. In a synchronic frame, we view language as a static system of relations. In a diachronic frame, we look at the historical processes of change that give rise to the synchronic relations observed. But if you look at the dynamic nature of language you will quickly see that diachrony – in the usual sense of the development and divergence of languages through social history – is not the only dynamic frame.

Vygotsky distinguished between *phylogenetic*, *ontogenetic*, and *historical* processes, and stressed that these dynamic frames were distinct from each other yet interconnected. His insight has been echoed and developed, from psychologists of communication like Tomasello (1999) and Cole (2007) to computational linguists like Steels (1998, 2003) and Smith et al. (2003).

Smith et al. (2003: 540) argue that to understand language we have to see it as emerging out of the interaction of multiple complex adaptive systems. They name three "time scales" that need to be taken into account – *phylogenetic*, *ontogenetic*, and *glossogenetic* (= "cultural evolution", i.e., diachronic) – thus echoing Vygotsky. Language is, they write, "a consequence of the interaction between biological evolution, learning and cultural evolution" (Smith et al. 2003: 541). Rączaszek-Leonardi focuses on psycholinguistic research, and proposes that three frames need to be addressed: *online*, *ontogenetic* and *diachronic*. She leaves out the phylogenetic frame, but adds the "online" frame of cognitive processing. Cole (1996: 185) expands the list of dynamic frames to include *microgenesis*,

2 Causal frames

ontogeny (distinguishing early learning from overall lifespan), *cultural history*, *phylogeny*, and even *geological time*. MacWhinney (2005: 193–195) offers a list of "seven markedly different time frames for emergent processes and structure", citing Tinbergen's mentor Konrad Lorenz (1958). MacWhinney's frames are *phylogenetic, epigenetic, developmental, processing, social, interactional*, and *diachronic*.

Newell (1990: 122) proposes a somewhat more mechanical division of time into distinct "bands of cognition" (each consisting of three "scales"). Newell takes the abstract/objective temporal unit of the second as a key unit, and defines each timescale on a gradient from 10^{-4} seconds at the fast end to 10^7 seconds at the slow end: the *biological band* (= 10^{-4}-10^{-2} seconds), the *cognitive band* (= 10^{-1}-10^1 seconds), the *rational band* (= 10^2-10^4 seconds), and the *social band* (= 10^5-10^7 seconds). He also adds two "speculative higher bands": the *historical band* (= 10^8-10^{10} seconds), and the *evolutionary band* (= 10^{11}-10^{13} seconds; Newell 1990: 152), thus suggesting a total of 18 distinct timescales.

Like Newell (though without reference to him), Lemke (2000: 277) takes the second as his unit and proposes no less than 24 "representative timescales", beginning with 10^{-5} seconds – at which a typical process would be "chemical synthesis" – through to 10^{18} seconds – the scale of "cosmological processes".

Lemke's discussion is full of insights. But he generates his taxonomy by arbitrarily carving up an abstract gradient. It is not established in terms of research-relevant qualitative distinctions or methodological utility, nor is it derived from a theory (cf. Uryu et al 2014, 2008: 169). It is not clear, for example, why a distinction between units of 3.2 years versus 32 years should necessarily correlate with a distinction between processes like institutional planning versus identity change; nor why the process of evolutionary change should span three timescales (3.2 million years, 32 million years and 317 million years) or why it should not apply at other timescales.

Larsen-Freeman & Cameron (2008: 169) propose a set of "timescales relevant to face-to-face conversation between two people": a *mental processing* timescale of milliseconds, a *microgenetic* timescale of online talk, a *discourse event* timescale, a *series of connected discourse events*, an *ontogenetic* scale of an individual's life, and a *phylogenetic* timescale. Uryu et al. (2014) critique this model for not explaining why these timescales are the salient or relevant ones, and for not specifying which other timescales are "real but irrelevant".

Uryu et al. (2014) propose a principled "continuum" of timescales running from "fast" to "slow" (11 distinctions in the order *atomic, metabolic, emotional, autobiographical, interbodily, microsocial, event, social systems, cultural, evolutionary, galactic*) that are orthogonal to a set of "temporal ranges" running from "simple" to "complex" (six distinctions in the order *physical universe, organic life forms, human species, human phenotype, dialogical system, awareness*). Uryu et al's approach applies the notion of ecology to the dynamics of language and its usage (see also Cowley 2011, Steffensen & Fill 2014).

What to make of this array of multi-scale schemes? Some are well-motivated but incomplete. Saussure gives a single dynamic frame, leading us to wonder, for example, whether we should regard speech processing as nano-diachrony. Vygotsky gives us three dynamic frames, but does not single out or sub-distinguish "faster" frames like microgeny and enchrony. Are we to think of these as pico-ontogeny? On the other hand, some schemes give us finer differentiation than we need, or offer arbitrary motivations for the distinctions made. What we need is a middle way.

2.2 MOPEDS: A basic-level set of causal frames

Of the frames discussed in the previous section, six capture what is most useful about previous proposals. These six frames are relatively well understood. They are known to be relevant to research. They are well-grounded in prior work on language and culture. And they are known to be related to each other in interesting ways.[1] This is what we need: a basic-level set of conceptually distinct but interconnected causal frames for understanding language.

Each of the six frames – microgenetic, ontogenetic, phylogenetic, enchronic, diachronic, synchronic – is distinct from the others in terms of the kinds of causality it implies, and thus in its relevance to what we are asking about language and its relation to culture and other aspects of human diversity. One way to think about these distinct frames is that they are different sources of evidence for explaining the things that we want to understand. I now briefly define each of the six frames.

2.2.1 Microgenetic (action processing)

In a microgenetic frame, we look at how language and culture are psychologically processed. For example, in order to produce a simple sentence, a person goes through a set of cognitive processes including concept formulation, lemma

---

[1] One might wonder if one or more of these frames might be reduced in terms of one or more others. It is reminiscent of the idea of reducing social processes to physical ones: Were such a reduction possible, it is unlikely to be helpful.

retrieval, and phonological encoding (Levelt 1989). Or when we hear and understand what someone says (Cutler 2012), we have to parse the speech stream, recognize distinct words and constructions, and infer others' communicative intentions.

These processes tend to take place at time scales between a few milliseconds and a few seconds. Causal mechanisms at this level include working memory (Baddeley 1986), rational heuristics (Gigerenzer et al. 2011), minimization of effort (Zipf 1949), categorization, motor routines, inference, ascription of mental states such as beliefs, desires, and intentions (Searle 1983; Enfield & Levinson 2006), and the fine timing of motor control and action execution.

2.2.2 Ontogenetic (biography)

In an ontogenetic frame, we look at how a person's linguistic habits and abilities are learned and developed during the course of that person's lifetime. Many of the things that are studied within this frame come under the general headings of language acquisition and socialization. This refers to both the learning of a first language by infants (see Clark 2009, Brown & Gaskins 2014) and the learning of a second language by adults (Klein 1986).

The kinds of causal processes seen in the ontogenetic frame include strategies for learning and motivations for learning. Some of these strategies and motivations can be complementary, and some may be employed at distinct phases of life. Causal processes involved in this frame include conditioning, statistical learning and associated mechanisms like entrenchment and pre-emption (Tomasello 2003), adaptive docility (Simon 1990), a pedagogical stance (Gergely & Csibra 2006), and long-term memory (Kandel 2009).

2.2.3 Phylogenetic (biological evolution)

In a phylogenetic frame we ask how our species first became able to learn and use language. This is part of a broader set of questions about the biological evolution and origin of humankind. It is a difficult topic to study, but this has not stopped a vibrant bunch of researchers from making progress (Hurford 2007, 2012; Levinson 2014).

Causal processes in a phylogenetic frame include those typically described in evolutionary biology. They invoke concepts like survival, fitness, and reproduction of biological organisms (Ridley 1997, 2004), which in the case of language means members of our species. The basic elements of Darwinian natural selection are essential here: competition among individuals in a population, conse-

2.2 MOPEDS: A basic-level set of causal frames

quential variation in individual characteristics, heritability of those characteristics, exaptation, non-telic design, and so forth (Darwin 1859; Dawkins 1976; Jacob 1977; Mayr 1982).

2.2.4 Enchronic (social interactional)

In an enchronic frame, we look at language in the context of social interaction. When we communicate, we use sequences of moves made up of speech, gesture, and other kinds of signs. The causal processes of interest involve structural relations of sequence organization (practices of turn-taking and repair which organize our interactions; Schegloff 1968, 2007; Sacks et al. 1974; Schegloff et al. 1977; Sidnell & Stivers 2012) and ritual or affiliational relations of appropriateness, effectiveness, and social accountability (Heritage 1984; Atkinson & Heritage 1984; Stivers et al. 2011; Enfield 2013).

Turn-taking in conversation operates in the enchronic frame, as do speech act sequences such as question-answer, request-compliance, assessment-agreement, and suchlike (see Enfield & Sidnell 2014). Enchronic processes tend to take place at a temporal granularity around one second, ranging from fractions of seconds up to a few seconds and minutes (though as stressed here, time units are not the definitive measure; exchanges made using email or surface mail may stretch out over much greater lengths of time).

Enchronic processes and structures are the focus in conversation analysis and other traditions of research on communicative interaction. Some key causal elements in this frame include relevance (Garfinkel 1967; Grice 1975; Sperber & Wilson 1995), local motives (Schutz 1970; Leont'ev 1981; Heritage 1984), sign-interpretant relations (Kockelman 2005, 2013, Enfield 2013: Chapter 4), and social accountability (Garfinkel 1967; Heritage 1984).

2.2.5 Diachronic (social/cultural history)

In a diachronic frame, we look at elements of language as historically conventionalized patterns of knowledge and/or behavior. If the question is why a certain linguistic structure is the way it is, a diachronic frame looks for answers in processes that operate in historical communities. While of course language change has to be actuated at a micro level (Weinreich et al. 1968; Labov 1986; Eckert 2000), for a linguistic item to be found in a language, that item has to have been diffused and adopted throughout a community before it can have become a convention.

Among the causal processes of interest in a diachronic frame are the adoption and diffusion of innovations, and the demographic ecology that supports cultural transmission (Rogers 2003). Population-level transmission is modulated by microgenetic processes of extension, inference, and reanalysis that feed grammaticalization (Hopper & Traugott 1993).

Of central importance in a diachronic frame are social processes of group fission and fusion (Aureli et al. 2008), migration (Manning 2005), and sociopolitical relations through history (Smith 1776; Marx & Engels 1947; Runciman 2009). The timescales of interest in a diachronic frame are often stated in terms of years, decades, and centuries.

2.2.6 Synchronic (representation of relations)

Finally, a synchronic frame is different from the other frames mentioned so far because time is removed from consideration, or at least theoretically so. One might ask if it is a causal frame at all. But if we think of a synchronic system as a true description of the items and relations in a person's head, as coded, for example, in their memory, then this frame is real and relevant, with causal implications, even if we see it as an abstraction (e.g., as bracketing out near-invisible processes that take place in the fastest levels of Newell's "biological band"; see section 2.1, above).

In Saussure's famous comparison, language is like a game of chess. If we look at the state of the game half way, a diachronic frame would view the layout in terms of the moves that had been made up to that point, and that had created what we now see. A synchronic account would do no more than describe the positions and interrelations of the pieces on the board at that point in time. For an adequate synchronic description, one does not need to know how the set of relations came to be the way it is.

There are two ways to take this. One is to see the synchronic frame as a purely methodological move, an abstraction that allows the professional linguist to describe a language as a whole system that hangs together. Another – not in conflict with the first – is to see the synchronic description of a language as a hypothesis about what is represented in the mind of somebody who knows the language.

A synchronic system cannot be an entirely atemporal concept. At the very least this is because synchronic structures cannot be inferred without procedures that require time; e.g., the enchronic sequences that we use in linguistic elicitation with native speaker informants. But a synchronic system is clearly distinct from an associated set of ontogenetic processes, on the one hand, and diachronic processes, on the other (though it is causally implied in both). We can infer an adult's knowledge of language and distinguish this from processes including the learning that led to this knowledge and the history that created the conventional model for this knowledge (but which neither the learner nor the competent speaker need have had access to).

The goal here is to define frames that are relevant to a natural, causal account of language. So when I talk about a synchronic frame I mean a way of thinking about the conceptual representations of a language that make it possible for people to produce and interpret utterances in that language.

Causality in a synchronic frame is tied to events that led *to* the knowledge, and to events that may lead *from* it, as well as how the nature and value of one convention may be dependent on the nature and value of other conventions that co-exist as elements of the same system.

2.3 Interrelatedness of the frames

How are these frames interrelated? As Rączaszek-Leonardi (2010: 276) says, "even if a researcher aims to focus on a particular scale and system, he or she has to be aware of the fact that it is embedded in others". Other authors (Cole 1996: 179, MacWhinney 2005: 192) have asked: What are the forces that cause these frames to "interanimate" or "mesh"? The way to find out would be to test and extend the useful suggestions of authors like Newell (1990), Cole (1996: 184–185), MacWhinney (2005), Lemke (2000: 279–286) and Uryu et al. (2014).

How might the outputs of processes foregrounded within any one of these explanatory frames serve as inputs for processes foregrounded within any of the others? Answers to this question will greatly enrich our tools for explanation.

2.4 The case of Zipf's length-frequency rule

Why is it good to have a set of distinct causal frames for language? Because it offers explanatory power. Consider the observation made by Zipf that "every language shows an inverse relationship between the lengths and frequencies of usage of its words" (Zipf 1949: 66).[2] Zipf suggested that the correlation between word length and frequency is explained by a psychological preference for minimizing effort. If we take this as a claim that synchronic structures in language are caused by something psychological – though Zipf's own claims were rather more nuanced – this raises a linkage problem (Clark & Malt 1984: 201).

---

[2] I am grateful to Martin Haspelmath for insisting on the distinction between Zipf's Law and Zipf's length-frequency rule (cf. Newman 2005). Zipf's Law states that there is a correlation between the frequency of an item and its frequency rank relative to other items in a set. His length-frequency rule states that the shorter a word is, the more frequently the word is used.

2 Causal frames

The problem is that a person's desire to minimize effort cannot directly affect a synchronic system's structure. A cognitive preference is a property of an individual, while a synchronic fact is shared throughout a population. Something must link the two. While it may be true that the relative length of the words I know correlates with the relative frequency of those words, this fact was already true of my language before I was born. The correlation cannot have been caused by my cognitive preferences. How, then, can the idea be explicated in causal terms?

As was clear to Zipf (1949), to solve this problem we appeal to multiple causal frames. We can begin by bringing diachronic processes into our reasoning. A presumption behind an account like Zipf's is that all members of a population have effectively the same biases. The key to understanding the status of a microgenetic bias like "minimize effort in processing where possible" is to realize that this cognitive tendency has an effect only in its role as a *transmission bias* in a diachronic process of diffusion of convention in a historical population (see below chapters for explication of diachrony as an epidemiological process of biased transmission, following Rogers 2003, Sperber 1985, and Boyd and Richerson 1985; 2005). The synchronic facts are an aggregate outcome of individual people's biases multiplied in a community and through time. The bias has a causal effect precisely in so far as it affects the likelihood that a pattern will spread throughout that community.

Now, while the spread of a pattern and its maintenance as a convention in a group are diachronic processes, a transmission bias can operate in three other frames. In an ontogenetic frame, a correlation between the shortness of words and the frequency of words might make the system easier to learn. This bias causes the correlation to become more widely distributed in the population. In a microgenetic frame, people may want to save energy by shortening a word that they say often, again broadening the distribution of the correlation. And an enchronic frame will capture the fact that communicative behavior is not only regimented by individual-centered biases in learning, processing, and action, but also by the need to be successfully understood by another person if one's communicative action is going to have its desired effect. The presence of another person, who displays their understanding, or failure thereof, in a next move – criterial to the enchronic frame – provides a selectional counter-pressure against people's tendency to minimize effort in communicative behavior. One's action has to be recognized by another person if that action is going to succeed (Zipf 1949: 21, Enfield 2013: Chapter 9).

If we adopt a rich notion of a diachronic frame in which transmission biases play a central causal role, we can incorporate the ontogenetic, microgenetic and enchronic frames in explaining synchronic facts. We do this by invoking the mechanisms of *guided variation* explicated by Boyd & Richerson (1985, 2005) and explored in subsequent work by others (Kirby 1999; Kirby et al. 2004; Christiansen & Chater 2008; Chater & Christiansen 2010). This allows us to hold onto Zipf's insight, along with similar claims by authors such as Sapir before him, and Greenberg after him, who both also saw connections between individual-level psychological biases and community-level synchronic facts. Greenberg (1966) implied, for example, that there is a kind of cognitive harmony in having analogous structures in different parts of a language system. Sapir (1921: 154–158) suggested that change in linguistic systems by drift can cause imbalances and "psychological shakiness", which motivates the reorganization of grammar to avoid that mental discomfort.

Similar ideas can be found in work on grammaticalization (Givón 1984; Bybee 2010) and language change due to social contact (Weinreich 1953), leading to the same conclusion: Synchronic patterns can have psychological explanations but only when mediated by the aggregating force of diachronic processes.

The point is central to explaining other observed correlations in language and its usage, for example that more frequent words change more slowly (Pagel et al. 2007), that differences in processes of attention and reasoning correlate with differences in the grammar of the language one speaks (Whorf 1956; Lucy 1992; Slobin 1996), that ways of responding in conversation can be constrained by collateral effects of language-specific grammatical structures (Sidnell & Enfield 2012), that tendencies in natural meaning can correlate with universals in the sounds of words (Dingemanse et al. 2013), and that cultural values can shape grammatical categories (Hale 1986; Wierzbicka 1992; Chafe 2000; Enfield 2002; Everett 2005, 2012). But most if not all of these claims bracket out some elements of the full causal chain involved. To give a complete and explicit account, multiple frames are needed.

3 Transmission biases

Anyone who wants a natural, causal account of linguistic and other cultural transmission will have to study transmission biases. These are the biases that ultimately regulate the historical, cumulative transmission of culture. To understand how the linguistic habits of communities change over generations – in a diachronic frame – we must also look in the ontogenetic frame, that is, in the process of language acquisition, and the resultant slight differences in habits of speech between generations. Language acquisition involves the effective transmission of a language from parents to children. Imperfections in this transmission are sometimes thought to explain language change. Consistent patterns in the details of such changes have been documented across a wide range of the world's languages. Many argue that natural paths of semantic change are motivated by species-wide innate conceptual structure. There are universals in semantic change, independent from social factors and other factors outside the minds and bodies of speakers. But this is only part of the story. Even when new ideas for ways of saying things have their source within a single person, the spread of that idea follows mechanisms of population-level social transmission. And the success or failure of such transmission is ultimately dependent on the biases that are the topic of this chapter.

Cultural transmission can be usefully understood in relation to epidemiology (Dawkins 1976; Sperber 1985). We catch ideas from others, in this case ideas for attributing meanings to signs.

> An innovation in a language begins its existence in the mouths and minds of one or more speakers and spreads from them to other speakers. In fact, innovations occur constantly in the speech of individuals, but an innovation becomes part of the history of the language only when it spreads through the network to become a stable feature in the speech of a group of speakers. (Ross 1997: 214–215)

On syntax specifically, Harris and Campbell make a similar point:

> Isolated creative, exploratory expressions are made constantly by speakers of all ages. Such expressions may be developed for emphasis, for stylistic

> or pragmatic reasons (to facilitate communication as in changes to avoid ambiguity or to foster easier identification of discourse roles), or they may result from production errors. The vast majority of such expressions are never repeated, but a few "catch on". (Harris & Campbell 1995: 54)

How do they catch on? How do they make this leap from single speaker to population-wide? How does an innovation become a stable feature in the speech of a group of speakers? In this chapter I discuss a crucial part of the answer to this question: the *biases* that operate in linguistic and cultural change, in the diachronic frame. I will define some important biases, and I will say why we need a coherent conceptual framework to explain just why we observe the biases we observe.

3.1 Cultural epidemiology

In the cultural evolution of language, that is, the diffusion, maintenance, and change of linguistic practices in historical communities, it is often assumed or implied that the unit of analysis is the language system as a whole. But the diachronic replication and transmission of whole language systems is not causally conducted directly at the system level (see Chapter 1 above). It is an aggregate outcome of a massive set of much simpler and much smaller concrete speech events that operate, in enchronic and microgenetic frames, on the *parts* of a language, such as words or pieces of grammar (Hudson 1996).

Language systems only exist because populations of linguistic items replicate and circulate in human communities, whenever people say things. A causal account of language evolution that focuses on the transmission of linguistic items can be called an epidemiological view, following Sperber (1985, 1996), and in a similar spirit to Keller (1994) and Croft (2000). In an item-based account, the pieces of a system can change independently from other pieces, and they can be plucked out and borrowed from one system to another. This happens for example when we borrow a word. In diachronic processes, both enchronic and microgenetic processes play a role.

Ultimately we need a causal account for why it sometimes seems like we can treat languages as if they were organism-like systems (e.g., when we write grammars). This is the topic of Chapter 4, below. But first we need to define the basic underlying causal anatomy of item-based language transmission. Here I outline the basics of a transmission biases approach to the historical evolution of languages.

3.2 Biased transmission

The diffusion of cultural items in the diachronic frame is explained in terms of a *biased transmission* model of the distribution of cultural knowledge and practice within human populations and across generations, following a general framework of cultural epidemiology (Sperber 1985, 1996; Boyd & Richerson 1985, 2005; Enfield 2003, 2008). In a biased transmission model, the question of whether fashions of cultural practice in a population spread, decline, transform, or remain as they are will be determined by the cumulative effect of biases: filters, pumps, and transformers on cultural practices in a competition for social uptake. The processes are visible in the diachronic frame, but their proximal causal bases are seen in enchronic and microgenetic frames.

Linguistic and other cultural items are not confined to the mind. Nor are they confined to things or actions that can be perceived. They are simultaneously manifest in mental *and* material domains, *and* in relations between these domains. At any moment, a community is buzzing with enchronic and microgenetic causal chains that constitute continuous lines of production and comprehension of pieces of language and culture. I am referring to people's courses of goal-directed action using words, tools, body movements, and other cultural items.

These courses of behavior are contexts in which the natural histories of cultural and linguistic items are played out. They constitute causal chains with links from mind (I know a word, I understand a tool) to usage (I use the word in conversation, I use the tool for a purpose), to mind (the other person learns or recognizes the word, an onlooker learns or recognizes the tool's function, attributing a goal to my behavior), to usage, to mind, to usage, to mind, to usage, and so on. This type of causal trajectory is a chain of *iterated practice*, or a cognitive causal chain (Sperber 2006). See Figure 3.1 for a simplified illustration.

Figure 3.1: Simplified illustration of iterated practice, or a social cognitive causal chain (Sperber 2006:438).

Figure 3.1 is not an *iterated learning* chain, of the kind presented by Kirby and colleagues (Kirby et al. 2004, 2008), among others (Christiansen & Chater 2008; see below). Those iterated learning depictions resemble Figure 3.1, but they are not the same. In iterated learning (studied to date using small, artificial languages in lab settings), each arrow from public to private may represent an entire learning process in an ontogenetic frame, such as a child's learning of a language. Each link in the chain is effectively a single macro-level state change in ontogeny (e.g., the move from not knowing the language to knowing the language). This is shorthand for a huge set of small events and small associated state changes.

Learning a language involves not one event but many iterations of exposure and reproduction. In each micro-occasion of exposure and reproduction there is feedback that comes from others' reactions to how we use words in context. This feedback plays an essential role in learning. Both the microgenetic and ontogenetic frames are relevant. The iterated learning model abstracts away from these details (not without practical reason), while the iterated practice model in Figure 3.1 tries to capture them directly and explicitly.

While iterated learning focuses on the ontogenetic or biographical frame, iterated practice focuses on the enchronic frame, that is, the frame of moves and counter-moves in human interaction (see Enfield 2009: 10, 2013: Chapter 4). In Figure 3.1, each link in the chain from private-public-private does not represent a generation of individuals in a human population (by contrast with the comparable figure in Christiansen & Chater 2008). It represents a generation of individuals in a population of items, that is, one local cycle of instantiation of a practice, such as a single use of a word, a single performance of a ritual, or a single occasion of making bacon and eggs for breakfast.

The schema in Figure 3.1 draws our attention to a set of bridges that a bit of culture has to cross if it is to survive a cycle of iterated practice. What are the forces that help things across those bridges, and what are the forces that inhibit them? These forces are called transmission biases (following Boyd & Richerson 1985, 2005). This kind of account assumes a standard model of Darwinian evolution – variation of heritable traits in a population – where the variation is guided in a specific way.

As Boyd & Richerson (1985) formulate it, variation of cultural items is guided by the properties of people. For example, if a certain way of doing something is easier to learn than some other functionally equivalent way (e.g., doing mathematics on a calculator versus on an abacus), then this is likely to increase the frequency of the easier variant in the population. All things being equal, this variant will also in turn become more frequent simply because it is already more frequent.

Christiansen & Chater (2008) use this idea in arguing that the properties of the human brain, e.g., for learning and processing language, favour certain linguistic variants over others. Language is the way it is because it is "shaped by the brain", and thus not because the evolution of a language faculty has caused the human brain to change in some fundamental way as a result of the way language is.

Assuming this model of guided variation, the question then becomes: What are the forces that guide variation in this way, and that operate upon variants within a population, ultimately determining whether those variants become, or remain, conventional in the population? We now consider some known biases.

3.3 Some known biases

Variants of cultural behavior compete for adoption by people in populations. Different researchers have described different biases, sometimes in quite specific terms, sometimes in general terms.

Christiansen and Chater (2008; see also Chater & Christiansen 2010) describe four factors that mostly have to do with properties of the individual human body, especially the brain. These are (1) perceptuo-motor factors, (2) cognitive limitations on learning and processing, (3) constraints from mental representations, (4) pragmatic constraints. These factors can affect the likelihood that one linguistic variant is selected over another. (The social mechanisms that are also a necessary part of the process are left implicit by these authors.)

Boyd & Richerson (1985) introduce distinctions that are broader in kind. They illustrate with an example from table tennis. For the function of hitting the ball, you can choose between holding the bat with a pencil grip or a handle grip. Choosing one of these variants necessarily rules out choosing the other. They discuss biases that might cause a person to select one or the other grip.

A *direct bias* has to do with the relationship between a variant and a person who adopts that variant. It concerns affordances (Gibson 1979). A person should choose variant A if it is somehow more advantageous than variant B for a proximate function in some context. By a direct bias we should choose the grip that is easier, more effective, feels better, gives better results.

An *indirect bias* has to do with social identity. When a person adopts a variant, other people will see. This will lend a certain status to both the adopter (as the kind of person who adopts that variant) and the variant (as a variant that is adopted by that person or someone like that). People adopt variants of behaviors not only for their efficacy but also with some idea of how they will be seen by others when they make that choice. So by an indirect bias we should choose the same grip as people who we identify with, or want to emulate.

Finally, a *frequency-dependent bias* favours variants that are more frequent.

3 Transmission biases

Similar biases have been described in a large literature in sociology on the diffusion of innovations (Rogers 2003). Here, we can discern three sets of conditioning or causal factors in the success or failure of a practice.

1. *Sociometric factors* have to do with the network structure of demographic groups. People are socially connected in different ways, especially in terms of the number of their points of connection to others in a social network, as well as the quality of these connections. A practice is more likely to spread if it is modeled by someone who is widely connected in a network. This is because he or she will expose a greater number of people to the practice. Gladwell (2000) refers to this as the law of the few: a small number of people in group have the biggest influence on the diffusion of innovation.

2. *Personality factors* have to do with differences between people in the population that can affect the success or failure of an innovation. Some people are more willing than others to innovate and to adopt others' innovations (early adopters versus laggards). These differences may correlate with social categories such as age, class, and sub-culture. Some people are better known or better admired in their social milieu and may thus be more likely to be imitated.

3. The *utility* of an innovation is more or less what Boyd & Richerson (1985) refer to as direct bias, outlined above. The innovation will take off if it is more advantageous to potential adopters.

Each of the biases we have just reviewed plays an important role in the mechanisms of transmission that drive the circulation of bits of culture in human populations. But how to explain them? Where do these biases come from and how are they related to each other? Can we motivate these biases by locating them directly in the causal anatomy of transmission?

3.4 A scheme for grounding the biases

One way to justify and limit the number of transmission biases is to motivate them in terms of the structure of iterated practice shown in Figure 3.1. This structure gives us a way of locating and characterizing the biases. If we look at the elements of transmission illustrated in Figure 3.1, we see at the heart of it a repeating, four-stroke cycle consisting of the following steps (see Figure 3.2):

3.4 A scheme for grounding the biases

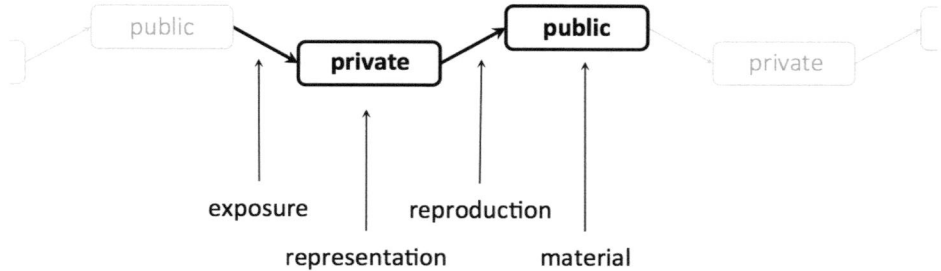

Figure 3.2: Loci for transmission biases; a four-stroke engine model.

1. *Exposure*: a process of going from public (out in the world) to private (in someone's mind), when a person comes into contact with, and perceives or engages with, a bit of culture;

2. *Representation*: how an idea is created and stored in the mind, based on (1), and the private product of this process;

3. *Reproduction*: a process of going from private (in someone's mind) to public (out in the world), made possible in part by a person's motivation to cause the same public event as in (1).

4. *Material*: the physical result of an event of reproduction of a cultural item.

5. Stages (3–4) can then lead to another round by exposing another person to the cultural item in question (feeding into a new stage (1)).

Each of the four steps is a possible threshold for any bit of culture to succeed or fail in the competition for uptake in a community. If people aren't exposed to it, it will die. If it is difficult to remember or think of, or if in the course of mental representation it is radically altered, it will die, or effectively die. If people aren't motivated to reproduce it, no further exposure will happen, and when the people who have learned the practice in question die, the practice will die with them. This happens for example with language extinction. And if the practice is not physically realized, so that others may perceive it, the transmission process will stall.

Failure on any of these four loci of transmission causes a break in the chain and may cause the variant to no longer exist.

Do not get the impression that a single such chain represents the entire historical trajectory of a cultural item. It is only the tiniest strand. At any moment, there is a thicket of equivalent chains of iterated practice that keep a bit of language or culture alive and evolving in a community.

Again, the question that a biased transmission approach to linguistic epidemiology asks is: What are the filters, pumps, and transformers that act upon the history of a cultural item? On the present proposal, we can posit four functionally-defined loci at which any bias can have an effect. Each locus is defined by the function it serves in braking, accelerating, or altering the transmission of practices in communities through social-cultural interaction, in an enchronic frame.

While there may be a long, if not open list of possible biases, they all should be definable in terms of how they operate upon one or more of the four transmission loci, exhaustively defined by the causal structure represented in Figures 3.1 and 3.2 above: *exposure* (world-to-mind transition), *representation* (mind structure), *reproduction* (mind-to-world transition), and *material* (world structure). Within the framework of these basic causal loci for transmission (1–4), different biases may affect the transmission of a practice in different ways.

As sketched above, some of these biases will have to do with facts about social networks, some with individual personality traits, some with properties of human perception, attention, memory, and action, some with the shape of the human body, some with the culture-specific means and ends that come with culturally evolved structures of activity, some with the organization of complex information in cognition. Let us now briefly consider how the previously described biases fit within the framework of these minimal loci for cultural transmission. Before we start, here is an important point. The goal of this exercise is not to locate each bias at just one point in the chain. As we shall see, some biases have effects at more than one point. This is one of the things the exercise shows us.

3.4.1 Exposure

Exposure – relating to the world-to-mind transition – is where biases can affect the likelihood that a person will come into contact with, and pay attention to, a practice.

One type of bias that effects exposure is social connectedness. All people are situated in social networks, but they are situated in different ways. One type of difference between people has to do with the number of other people we come into contact with. *Connectors* have a large number of social ties (Granovetter 1973). They are more likely to be exposed to an innovation, or to expose others to it. People with fewer social network connections will have a lower chance of being exposed to a given practice, or exposing others.

Another type of bias relevant to exposure is salience. When you come across a new kind of behavior you may or may not pay attention to it. The things that stand out will more likely to attract your attention. The definition of "stand out" is clearly a matter of perception in the classical sense of affordances, that is, a matter of the *relationship between* a person and a thing being perceived. Some things are more likely to be noticed because of the nature of our senses in relation to the world. Other things are more salient to us because we are actively looking for them, often because our language or culture encourages or requires it.

A third bias relevant to exposure is identity. Who is the person carrying out the practice when it is encountered? If it is somebody who I want to be like in some way, then I am more likely to pay attention to what the person is doing and how. If it is someone I have no interest in, I will be less likely to pay attention. In this way, social identity can play a role in biasing exposure, by affecting the extent to which someone will attend, or carefully attend, to the practice when encountered.

3.4.2 Representation

Representation – relating to mind structure – is where biases can affect the likelihood that, or the manner in which, a practice will be learnt or stored by a person, or how the psychological or otherwise private component of a practice will be structured.

Once we are exposed to a certain pattern of behavior, we can learn it. We form a representation of it, attributing to it some meaning or function, and we incorporate that representation into an existing framework of knowledge.

Some innovations are more memorable than others. Some things are more easily internalized. This is explained by cognitive preferences that are either known from psychological science or that are on that research agenda.

There are other differences in how things are learnt. Whether you see a thing, hear it, feel it, or some combination of these, can have consequences for how that thing is interpreted, learnt and understood (Enfield 2009: Chapter 6). This can then affect how the new knowledge is applied. For example, it may shape how you decide that a practice is an appropriate means for certain ends in a particular context.

There are effects of the psychological context into which a practice is embedded. Practices are partly constituted by knowledge; knowledge that is caused by, and in turn causes, public behavior and associated states of affairs. Knowledge has structure, including part-whole relations, hierarchical relations, and other sorts of dependency among items in a system.

When we learn something, we relate it to other things we know. We do this at the very least because the thing stood in a certain relation to other things in the context in which we learnt it. As an example, if I learn a new word such as *deplane*, I relate it to other words I already know. There might be similarities with other words: *debone, derail, decode, decommission.* Or associations with other features of the language system: *deplane* is a verb and can be used only with specific grammatical roles in English sentences. Or if I learn about the possibility of downloadable ringtones I will naturally link this to my existing knowledge of mobile phones and the Internet. All of these are examples of a *context bias*. Through a context bias a person is more readily able to learn and psychologically represent those things that have an existing "place" in which to fit.

In language, items are structured into paradigms, syntagms, conceptual frames, semantic fields, and other kinds of linguistic systems. While these systems often display a degree of symmetry, consistency, and simplicity, change is always taking place. In a system, when something happens in one place this will have effects in another place. In lexicon and grammar, such system-internal dynamics can give rise to a certain "psychological shakiness", as Sapir (1921) put it. As noted already in Chapter 2 above, this can lead to reorganization of a system, in people's heads, and then potentially in a whole community.

Now finally, note that *content biases* are also relevant to the representation locus of transmission. In the broadest sense of meaning, capturing everything from the arbitrary meanings of words in languages to the affordance-grounded functions of tools (Kockelman 2006), we benefit from what can be called natural meaning. If a word or grammatical expression is compatible with other information, for example by having iconic properties, it is better learnt and remembered. Similarly for technology, if there is a good match between the intended function of a tool and the tool's natural affordances, then we are more likely to understand the practice of using that tool, it will be easier to learn, and indeed what needs to be stored in the mind is reduced because the relevant information can stored materially (Norman 1991). These examples of the content bias pertain to learning, storage, and reduction of load on cognition.

3.4.3 Reproduction

Reproduction – relating to the mind-to-world transition – is where biases can affect the likelihood that a person who is exposed to a kind of behavior will later do it themselves. One way to think of this sense of reproduction is whatever causes a person to turn the private representation of a practice into an action whose production and effects are then perceptible by others.

What motivates us to turn knowledge into action? Daily life involves goal-directed behavior that is motivated by our beliefs and desires (Davidson 2006; Searle 1983; Fodor 1987). I may want to get something done for which I need another person's cooperation. One way to do this is with language. I select certain words and grammatical constructions as tools for the job. Depending on my goals, I will choose certain words and will thereby choose against all the other words I could have used.

This is the competition among words and grammatical forms invoked in Darwin's (1871: 60) citation of Max Müller (1870): "A struggle for life is constantly going on amongst the words and grammatical forms in each language". The competition among different cultural practices operates in the same way. Suppose I have a goal. I will have beliefs about how it can be attained. I will have knowledge that allows me to act. I can foresee at least some effects of my actions. All this points to a powerful bias at the reproduction locus of transmission, concerning a person's functional needs, and the available means to those ends.

The content bias, again, fits partly under this rubric. As discussed above, a content bias favours a practice that is more beneficial in some way to the person who selects it. Recall that a direct content bias applies when the benefit is greater functional payoff, or reduced cost, of the practice, in terms of its primary functional effects. In the table tennis example (see section 3.3, above), a direct content bias would favour the pencil grip if the pencil grip were lower in cost or greater in benefit than the handle grip – that is, in terms of its efficacy for getting the ball back over the net and, ultimately, for winning matches. An indirect content bias is also relevant to the reproduction locus of transmission: the choice to use the variant at all will have to do with the effects of whom you might show yourself to identify with (or against). There is an extensive literature on this in sociolinguistics. Speaking English, I might say *guy* in one context and *bloke* in another. Maybe there is a slight meaning difference between these two words, thus invoking a direct content bias. But these differences may be minimal compared to the effect of identifying myself with certain sub-cultural groups or kinds of social relationship by virtue of this choice between different word forms with near-identical meanings.

Clearer examples concern pronunciation. Whether I choose to say *working* or *workin'* has more to do with who I want to identify with (an indirect bias) rather than the meaning I want to convey (a direct bias). In the cultural realm, both a Rolex and a Tagheuer will tell the time for a high price but the choice to wear one or the other may depend on whether you want to identify with Roger Federer versus Tiger Woods (or tennis versus golf).

And there is perhaps most often some combination of the two. Do I choose to drink this brand of beer over all the rest because it tastes better (a direct bias) or because by doing so I identify with some person or group of people (an indirect bias)? It could be both. In any case, the mechanisms at play will bias a person's motivation for selecting one practice over all the others that he thereby does not select.

The indirect bias is also sometimes called a model bias. An important distinction can be made here depending on the age of the person concerned. How does a child select which variants of a practice to adopt? A conformity bias favours those practices that "everyone else" adopts (Boyd & Richerson 1985; Gergely & Csibra 2006). Another term for this bias is docility (Simon 1990). This refers to an adaptive propensity to do what other members of your group do, and in the same ways, without wondering why. An infant's model group will tend also to consist of the people who she is genetically most closely related to. The effect is that cultural practices and genes tend to (but need not) have parallel histories.

As people grow up and come to be regarded full members of their group, they come across a greater number and range of cultural items. They keep learning. So at any time they may find themselves with new choices. This may be because they encounter other ways of doing things than the way "my people" do things. This happens when they come into contact with other groups, for instance in trading, ritual and other kinds of inter-group social interaction. Different people in a community will have different degrees of mobility, sometimes as a result of personality, sometimes as a result of gender (men often travel more widely than women), age or sub-culture.

At a later age, there is a greater degree of choice and therefore greater competition between choices. We may or may not consciously deliberate about such choices. But as adults we may be more aware of the meanings of different options. Here is where the indirect bias looks more like the model bias exploited in commercial advertising. This bias applies in all diffusional processes by favouring practices that are modeled by, for example, more admired or charismatic people.

3.4.4 Material

Material – relating to world structure – is where biases can affect the way in which a practice will be physically perceived.

Biases on the material locus of transmission have to do with the physical affordances of cultural practices, and the ways in which these affordances affect the exposure and reproduction of those practices. Material-related biases can affect exposure-related biases in some obvious ways. The material nature of speech is such that it fades almost instantly (gesture slightly less so, etc; see Enfield 2009). But when language is reproduced in writing, this evanescence is dramatically lessened, and the dynamics of transmission are significantly affected.

Outside of language, we see similar contrasts. Many activities, like adopting a certain grip for table tennis, can only be seen momentarily. They are only available for exposure simultaneously with the reproduction process that potentially constitutes the transmission event (photos, etc., aside). The table tennis bat itself, however, has a more persistent physical existence, and can stand as a public sign for the possible ways people might handle it (Norman 1988; Kockelman 2006).

Material-related biases have to do with the ways in which cultural practices are made public, and how their form of public existence might affect their availability in the exposure-reproduction cycle we have been exploring here.

3.4.5 Networks

If the above-mentioned elements are an engine for the transmission of innovation, then social networks are the paths that innovations take. The career of an idea may theoretically be mapped in a large but finite network (Luce 1950, Miller 1951: Chapter 12, Milroy 1980; Ross 1997).

In fashion and other kinds of social epidemic, the success of an innovation will partly depend on the ways in which people's personalities differ. As Gladwell (2000) accessibly lays out, different personality types contribute to the diffusion of innovation in complementary ways. Connectors have a high number of weak social connections, in a range of social spheres. Mavens are actively interested in the market, and want to share their knowledge and opinions. Salesmen are the charismatic, persuasive ones who model innovations and effectively sell them. Innovators are the risk-takers who try things before anyone else does. They are followed by early adopters, the early majority, the more conservative late majority, and finally, the laggards.

When all of these types of people come into contact, they form social networks. The approach to language in terms of networks was pioneered in sociolinguistics by Milroy (1980), and also taken up by Le Page & Tabouret-Keller (1985), Ross (1997), and others. Milroy (1980) developed a method for studying linguistic variation based around the idea of social networks, "the informal social relationships contracted by an individual" (Milroy 1980: 174), which "can be used to account for variability in *individual* linguistic behavior in communities" (Milroy 1980: 21). The social network model "treats speakers as nodes in a social network, such that each speaker is connected with other speakers by social (and therefore communication) links" (Ross 1997: 213). The idea is to map the network of contacts that each individual has. Milroy suggested that networks could be placed on a scale of density, from low to high. In a low density network, *a* may be in regular contact with *b, c,* and *d,* but *b, c,* and *d* are never in contact with each other. In a high density network, *a, b, c,* and *d* are all in contact with each other.

Usually, contacts between two people are made in the presence of other network members. So, to the high density network, we could add the ties *a-b-c, a-b-d, a-c-d, b-c-d,* and *a-b-c-d*.

The network concept contributes "to analysis of the manner in which individuals utilize the resources of linguistic variability available to them." (Milroy 1980: 175). In work with Li on the topic of code-switching, Milroy writes:

> (A) network analysis can... form an important component in an integrated social theory of language choice. It links the community with the interactional level in focusing on everyday behavior of social actors. ... The link with the economic and sociopolitical level derives from the observation that networks seem to form not arbitrarily but in response to social and economic pressures. (Milroy & Li 1995: 155)

While "density" refers to the intensity of contact among network members, there are distinctions in the quality of relationships between any two network members. A distinction between *exchange* and *interactive* networks was suggested by Milardo (1988), to which Milroy and Li add *passive* network ties:

> Exchange networks constitute persons such as kin and close friends with whom ego not only interacts routinely, but also exchanges direct aid, advice, criticism, and support – such ties may therefore be described as "strong". Interactive networks on the other hand consist of persons with whom ego interacts frequently and perhaps over prolonged periods of time, but on whom ego does not rely for personal favours and other material or symbolic resources – such ties may be therefore described as "weak". An example of an interactive tie would be that between a shop-owner and a customer. In addition to exchange and interactive ties, we identified a "passive" type of network tie, which seemed particularly important to migrant families. Passive ties entail an absence of regular contact, but are valued by ego as a source of influence and moral support. Examples are physically distant relatives or friends. (Milroy & Li 1995: 138–139)

The key point is that sociolinguistics and network analysis give us a valuable matrix in which a four-stroke diffusion engine operates, modulated as it is by transmission biases (see especially Rogers 2003 for a rich review of cases and analyses of the diffusion of social innovation).

3.5 Causal anatomy of transmission

A causal explanation of linguistic reality must include the role of transmission biases in the diffusion of innovations in social networks. A good diachronic account of language change must be explicit about the proximal causal anatomy of the process, operating in microgenetic, enchronic, and ontogenetic frames. Previous work has usefully identified and described transmission biases, but one might ask: Why these biases? What other biases might we predict are possible? How many might there be?

We can answer these questions with reference to the basic, proximal causal anatomy of social transmission. It is powered by a four-stroke engine, a causal chain in the enchronic frame, from exposure to representation to replication to material instantiation, back to exposure and round again. A transmission bias is any force that serves as a filter, pump, or transformer for this process, with effects on any of the links in the potentially open-ended chain of iterated practice.

A next step is to see how well we can explain the known and understood biases within this four-stroke engine framework, and to see what predictions can be made and tested. This should connect to research on the puzzle of how our species evolved the capacity for cumulative culture (Tomasello 1999), a capacity that is strongly pronounced in humans but weak if present at all in our closest relatives, the other apes (Herrmann et al. 2007). While we can readily assume that other animals are engaged in goal-directed courses of action, and that they select from among different means for fixed ends in both the social and material realms, their selection of means for ends is relatively less flexible than that of humans. What is the link to transmission biases? We might assume that a chimpanzee, say, will be guided in its selection of a behavioral strategy by a strong content bias, incorporating a basic min-max payoff logic: keep effort to a minimum while ensuring the desired outcome. But if its repertoire of strategies is, on the whole, not being acquired by learning from others – but, say, learned by ritualization during the course of life, in an ontogenetic frame – then transmission biases will have no traction.

4 The item/system problem

When accounts of social-cultural transmission are explicit about the causal processes involved, they often take cultural *items* – rather than systems – as their unit of analysis. This works well but it is awkward because we know that cultural items don't exist in isolation. We can only make sense of cultural items in the context of a *system* of cultural meaning. This brings us back to the puzzle, foreshadowed in Chapter 1, of causal units.

Higher-level systems like languages and cultures show enormous coherence of structure, so much so that we are seduced into thinking of them as organisms with bodies (see classic statements of philologists von der Gabelentz 1891 and Meillet 1926: 16). Here is Gabelentz:

> Language is not a mere collection of words and forms, just as the organic body is not a mere collection of limbs and organs. Both are in any stage of their life (relatively) complete systems, dependent on themselves; all their parts are interdependent and each of their vital manifestations arises from this interaction. (von der Gabelentz 1891: 10)

Compare this to the situation in vertebrate biology. Genes are distinct entities yet they "form alliances" thanks to the bodies and body plans in which they are instantiated (Gould 1977, cited in Dawkins 1982: 117).

> Every gene in a gene pool constitutes part of the environmental background against which the other genes are naturally selected, so it's no wonder that natural selection favors genes that "cooperate" in building these highly integrated and unified machines called organisms. Biologists are sharply divided between those for whom this logic is as clear as daylight, and those (even some very distinguished ones) who just do not understand it – who naively trot out the obvious cooperativeness of genes and unitariness of organisms as though they somehow counted against the "selfish gene" view of evolution. ... By analogy with coadapted gene complexes, memes, selected against the background of each other, "cooperate" in mutually supportive memeplexes. (Dawkins 1999: xv)

4 The item/system problem

Vertebrates have bodies while cultural systems do not. Still, the item/system link needs to be accounted for in both cases. With both bodies and memeplexes, sets of items somehow hold together as systems. But the causal forces are different. The pieces of a cultural system are not held together at any stage by physical attachment to a shared material whole. So this is our puzzle. If languages and other cultural systems hang together, what is the binding force? We have seen that cultural transmission involves causal processes that apply only to small parts of the larger whole. What explains the coherence of that larger whole? This is the item/system problem.

Here is the solution. The ideas of cultural item and cultural system are reconciled by something that they have in common: Neither idea exists without the simpler idea of a *functional relation*. A word – kangaroo, for example – is easily thought of as a distinct cultural item. You can cite it or borrow it without having to also cite or borrow the language system that it comes from. But the word cannot be defined or understood – nor can it exist – except in terms of its functional relation to other things, things like the words it co-occurs with, the conversations in which it is used for referring to kangaroos, and so on. The same is true for technology. A spoke can be designed, named, bought, and sold, but as a cultural item, a spoke doesn't make sense without a wheel. And while a wheel is a whole when thought of with reference to a spoke, it is a *part* when thought of with reference to a vehicle, and so on.

In sum: An item doesn't make sense without functional relations to other things, just as a system doesn't make sense without the functional relations that it contains. Functional relations are the interface that joins items and systems together. We can look to functional relations for a solution to the item/system problem.

4.1 A transmission criterion

In the causal ontology of culture, there is a *transmission criterion*. A social fact – by definition – would cease to exist if individual people stopped behaving as if it existed (Searle 2010). And social facts endure with relative stability beyond individual people's lifetimes. Therefore, social facts must be transmitted among individuals in human populations in order to (i) exist and (ii) endure with relative stability. Transmission is a necessary part of what makes culture and language the way they are.

A causal understanding of culture depends, then, on knowing how culture is transmitted within human groups and across generations. Much is known about how *items* are transmitted (Rogers 2003), but macro-level cultural systems cannot be transmitted in the same way.

Do we need two separate accounts of transmission, one for items, one for systems? I am going to argue that we can derive system transmission from item transmission, on the condition that we have a more accurate definition of *items*. We can define items not as cultural things but as cultural things with functional relations to other cultural things. Cultural items are specified for – and advertize – their relations to the contexts into which they fit (where, it must be said, this fit can be quickly and easily re-tooled). As Kockelman (2013: 19) writes: "there are no isolated environments and organisms, there are only *envorganisms*."

4.2 Defining properties of systems

To understand what a cultural system is, begin with the idea of a cultural item. This is any seemingly detachable conceived entity such as a piece of technology, a technique, a way of saying something, a value. An item can be readily defined and labeled, and can be learned and borrowed from one human group into another (though typically with a change of meaning in the new context). Object-like things such as tomahawks might be prototypical items, but the idea of item intended here also includes train tracks, AC current, and mother-in-law avoidance.

By contrast, a cultural system is a coherent *set* of such items, each item related to the others. A system has a holism that goes beyond the sum of the parts, in the sense that the full meaning of any individual cultural item is determined by how it functions in relation to other things in context. Often, we cannot observe the system directly or in one go, as for example in the case of a language or a telecommunications infrastructure, though this is sometimes made virtually possible by means of *signs of* these systems that scale them down in such a way as to produce a "tangible expression", as Durkheim (1912: 208) put it, of the more diffuse phenomenon.

A book can contain a grammatical description of a language. A diagram can portray the elements of a telecommunications system in miniature. In these cases a representation of the system is created or inferred from an aggregate of encounters with context-situated items. These itemized emblems are different from the real systems they represent, and they have different collateral effects as a result of their form. A grammar book, for example, can be held up in one hand. This helps to promote the idea that a language is a finite, bounded thing; in short, an item.

4 The item/system problem

As we now turn to examine systems in more detail let me emphasize that neither items nor systems can be understood, nor indeed can they exist, without the *relations* that are inherent in both. Relations are definitive for both items and systems. If something is an item, relations define its *functions*. If it is a system, relations define its *structure*.

A system should have at least these three properties:

1. It can readily be construed as a thing with multiple inter-related parts.

2. Effects on one part should have effects on other parts.

3. The parts should together form a whole in the sense that they are more closely related to each other than they are to things outside the system.

Good examples are biological or ecological systems. In a food chain, populations of different species are inter-related. Changes in the frequency or behavior of one species will affect the frequency or behavior of others. While each species in the ecosystem will ultimately be connected to entities outside the focal food chain system, the integration *within* the system is greater.

Clearly, on all three counts, whether or not we are looking at a system is ultimately a matter of construal. To say that some entities form a system is partly just a way of looking at those entities.

4.3 Relations between relations

Culture and language hinge on shared meaning, and so the systems we are interested in here are *semiotic* systems. The core idea of a semiotic system is well illustrated in Darwin's account of the expression of emotion in animals. Darwin introduces a principle of *functional connection* between a sign and what it stands for.

In his example, the visible features of a dog in a "hostile frame of mind" – upright, stiff posture, head forward, tail erect and rigid, bristling hairs, ears forward, fixed stare – are intelligible because they recognizably "follow from the dog's intention to attack". Figure 4.1 is Darwin's illustration.

These behaviors are functionally connected to the aggressive attitude, and so others may take them to signal that attitude. This can be illustrated as in Figure 4.2.

This is only a first step toward establishing a semiotic system. Figure 4.2 shows a relatively simple semiotic relation. There is a potential positive association be-

4.3 Relations between relations

Figure 4.1: Darwin's illustration of a dog in hostile frame of mind (Figure 5 from *The Expression of the Emotions in Man and Animals*).

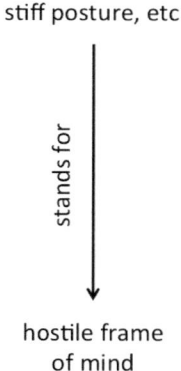

Figure 4.2: A "functional", indexical association between observable behavior and frame of mind (after Darwin).

4 The item/system problem

tween an observable behavior and a frame of mind. Whoever makes this association might produce a number of relevant interpretants, for example running away, grabbing a big stick, or adopting an attacking posture.

Darwin then argues for a second signalling principle, which he calls *antithesis*. The dog can exploit the already established semiotic relation shown in Figure 4.2 to express the *opposite* of aggression. He does this by "reversing his whole bearing", that is, doing the "opposite" of what he would do when aggressive. So, when approaching his master in an affectionate attitude, his visible behaviors will include body down, flexuous movements, head up, lowered wagging tail, smooth hair, ears loosely back, loose hanging lips, eyes relaxed. Figure 4.3 is Darwin's illustration.

Figure 4.3: Darwin's illustration of a dog in an affectionate attitude (Figure 6 from *The Expression of the Emotions in Man and Animals*).

> None of [these] movements, so clearly expressive of affection, is of the least direct service to the animal. They are explicable, as far as I can see, solely from being in complete opposition to the attitude and movements which are assumed when a dog intends to fight, and which consequently are expressive of anger. (Darwin 1872: 15–16)

As depicted in Figure 4.4, antithesis is a secondary relation. It is a relation between relations. As Darwin pointed out, this secondary relation is only possible if the interpreter has already recognized a primary functional relation. But there is something more that it depends on, something crucial to the idea of a semiotic system. It follows from the meaning of the term *opposite*.

4.3 Relations between relations

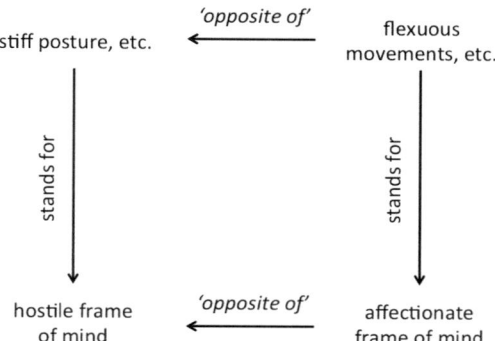

Figure 4.4: A secondary indexical association between observable behavior and frame of mind (at right), deriving its meaning only in connection with the established relation illustrated in Figure 4.2 (and incorporated at left of this Figure), assuming the interpreter's knowledge of a limited range of possible bodily behaviors, on the one hand, and a limited set of frames of mind, on the other (after Darwin).

To see that a certain behavior is "the opposite" of some other behavior, as opposed to simply *not* that other behavior, you must be able to consider alternative possibilities within a restricted set. Flexuous movements can be recognized as the opposite of the aggression-signaling behavior only when one knows, or can predict, a limited range of postures that a dog can make. For this to work in the way depicted in Figure 4.4, you must also understand that there is a limited set of relevant frames of mind that the dog may have, with aggressive at one end and affectionate at the other.

This type of semiotic system arises when Darwin's principle of antithesis sets up *relations between relations* (Kockelman 2013: 12–17). This becomes possible when someone has access not just to what they are currently perceiving (e.g., a dog in a certain posture) but when the person also knows about other systems such as body posture and emotional state, with some sense of their elements and the logical-causal relations between them. A person should understand that if a dog is being affectionate it is necessarily not being aggressive, or that if its body is stiff it cannot also be flexuous.

Central to the idea of a *functional relation to context* that I am outlining here are the concepts of *incorporation* and *contextualization*. These are defined in semiotic terms by Kockelman (2006: 29), as follows:

Incorporation. For any two semiotic processes, A and B, A will be said to incorporate B (and hence be an interpretant of it) if the sign of B relates to the sign of A as part-to-whole, and the object of B relates to the object of A as means-to-ends. For example, in the case of instruments (semiotic processes whose sign is an artificed entity and whose object is a function), a wheel incorporates a spoke.

Contextualization. For any two semiotic processes, A and B, A will be said to contextualize B, if A is required to interpret B, or at least assists in interpreting B. For example, a hammer contextualizes a nail. And a sword contextualizes a sheath. That is, nails make no sense without the existence of hammers; and sheaths make no sense without the existence of swords.

The concepts of incorporation and contextualization help us to define functional relations. They hold, for example, for the relations between a verb and a clause, a handle and a knife, a marriage rule and a kinship system. They account for relations between concepts and the larger frames that contextualize them (Fillmore 1982). They are the basis of combinatoric rules, and as such they ultimately account for grammar in the complete sense (assuming a semantically-based approach to grammar; cf. Langacker 1987; Wierzbicka 1988; Croft 2000; Haspelmath 2007).

4.4 More complex systems

The basic relations-between-relations structure shown in Figure 4.4 combines with incorporation and contextualization – kinds of embedding relations – to yield the sorts of semiotic systems that make up any natural language (Saussure 1916; see Dixon 2010, 2014, Bickel 2014).

All languages have systems of form classes. The thousands of words (and other morphemes) that you have to learn in order to speak a language can be categorized according to how they are distributed relative to each other. There are open classes of content words like nouns and verbs (in most if not all languages) versus closed classes of function words like prepositions (e.g., in English) and case-marking affixes (e.g., in Finnish).

Then there are constructional systems defined by principles of combination. An example is the system for describing motion events in Lao (Enfield 2007: 387–389). There are three consecutive slots. Each slot may be filled with a verb from three distinct sets. The first verb refers to the manner of motion (this is an open set). The second refers to the path of motion (from a set of 10 verbs). The third refers to the direction of motion in relation to the deictic center (from a set of 3 verbs). See Table 4.1.

Table 4.1: Lao directional verb system

Slot 1 Verb of manner (open class)	Slot 2 Verb of path (closed, n=10)	Slot 3 Verb of direction (closed, n=3)
lèèn1 'run' ñaang1 'walk' king4 'roll' lùan1 'slide' tên4 'jump' lòòj2 'float' khii1 'ride' khaan2 'crawl' taj1 'creep' com1 'sink' doot5 'leap' etc.	khùn5 'ascend' long2 'descend' khaw5 'enter' qòòk5 'exit' khaam5 'cross.over' lòòt4 'cross.under' taam3 'follow' phaan1 'pass' liap4 'go along edge' qòòm4 'go around'	paj3 'go' mùa2 'return' maa2 'come'

Using this system, a Lao speaker can say things like this:

(1) *khaan2 qòòk5 paj3*
    crawl   exit   go
    '(S/he/it) crawled out/away.'

(2) *doot5 long2   maa2*
    leap   descend come
    '(S/he/it) leapt down here.'

(3) *lòòj2 phaan1 mùa2*
    float pass   return
    '(S/he/it) floated back past.'

This linguistic sub-system illustrates a fundamental intersection between two axes. A *syntagmatic axis* is the "left-to-right" axis along which separate elements combine. On a *paradigmatic axis*, each slot along the syntagmatic axis may be

4 The item/system problem

filled by alternative members of a set, with contrast effects between possible values (not unlike the way a dog's stiff posture is opposed to a flexuous posture).

Sub-systems in language interact with each other and show dependencies in higher-level systems like those defined in comprehensive grammatical descriptions. Aikhenvald & Dixon (1998) describe dependencies among grammatical sub-systems. They point out, for example, that the system of polarity (positive versus negative in relation to a predicate or clause) puts constraints on other sub-systems in the grammars of many languages. For example, in Estonian, there is a system in which person and number are distinguished by morphological marking on the verbs, but these distinctions are only realized in positive polarity. The distinctions are lost in the negative. See Table 4.2.

Table 4.2: Verb 'to be' in Estonian

POSITIVE	NEGATIVE
olen (1SG), *oleme* (1PL)	
oled (2SG), *olete* (2PL)	*ei ole* (1/2/3SG/PL)
on (3SG/PL)	

Aikhenvald & Dixon (1998) present a cross-linguistic hierarchy of dependencies between sub-systems like these. This kind of inter-connectedness between paradigm sets and combinatoric rules, and between sub-systems in a language, is evidence for the broad underlying system properties of linguistic behavior.

It follows from these facts about linguistic systems that we cannot view any piece of language as a mere item. "A living language is not just a collection of autonomous parts", say Donegan & Stampe (1983: 1). A language is "a harmonious and self-contained whole, massively resistant to change from without, which evolves according to an enigmatic, but unmistakably real, inner plan" (Donegan & Stampe 1983: 1).

They illustrate their point in explaining how it is that the languages of two sides of the Austroasiatic language family – Munda and Mon-Khmer – show a list of typological distinctions that are "exactly opposite at every level of structure" (Donegan & Stampe 2002: 111) even though they are known to be descended from the same proto-language. Donegan and Stampe argue that speakers of Munda innovated a new prosodic profile, and when they did this they were tampering with something that "pervades every level of language structure" (Donegan & Stampe 1983: 14). A simple change from iambic to trochaic stress in words had systemic knock-on effects that changed the entire morphosyntactic profile of the language. Table 4.3 is adapted from Donegan & Stampe (1983: 1–2).[1]

Table 4.3: Properties of Munda and Mon-Khmer languages

	Munda	**Mon-Khmer**
Phrase accent	Falling (initial)	Rising (final)
Word order	Variable-SOV, AN, Postpositional	Rigid-SVO, NA, Prepositional
Syntax	Case, verb agreement	Analytic
Word canon	Trochaic, dactylic	Iambic, monosyllabic
Morphology	Agglutinative, suffixing, polysynthetic	Fusional, prefixing or isolating
Timing	Isosyllabic, isomoric	Isoaccentual
Syllable canon	(C)V(C)	Unaccented (C)V, accented (C)(C)V(G)(C)
Consonantism	Stable, geminate clusters	Shifting, tonogenetic, non-geminate clusters
Tone/register	Level tone (Korku only)	Contour tone/register
Vocalism	Stable, monophthongal, harmonic	Shifting, diphthongal, reductive

As the examples discussed here show, there are good reasons to believe that languages have higher-level system properties. Yet there is no single causal event in which a language as a whole system is transmitted, at least not in the same sense as the single causal event of sexual reproduction by which a full set of genetic information is transmitted in vertebrates. Below, I return to the transmission problem. But first, I want to broaden the scope and show that the point I have just made for language also holds for social and cultural systems.

---

[1] Donegan and Stampe of course considered the possibility that language contact explains the data in Table 4.3. Their goal was to argue against a contact account, with their knock-on effect idea being offered as an alternative. Whether they are right remains an open question. Neither contact nor internal development can be treated as a null hypothesis. Proponents of both arguments are obliged to make their case.

4 The item/system problem

As an illustration of the system concept in another domain of culture, consider *sections* and *subsections* in Aboriginal Australia (Radcliffe-Brown 1931). In a section system, all members of a community belong in one of four categories. Each category has a name in the local language (e.g., in the Alyawarre language of Central Australia they are *Kngwarriya, Upurla, Pitjarra* and *Kimarra*). For convenience we can label them A, B, C, and D.

As McConvell (1985: 2) describes it, in a four-term section system "a man of A marries preferentially a woman of B; their children are D. A man of B marries a woman of A; their children are C. C and D similarly marry each other, and their children are A if the mother is C and B if the mother is D". After two generations of this, one ends up in the same section as one's father's father or mother's mother. See Figure 4.5.

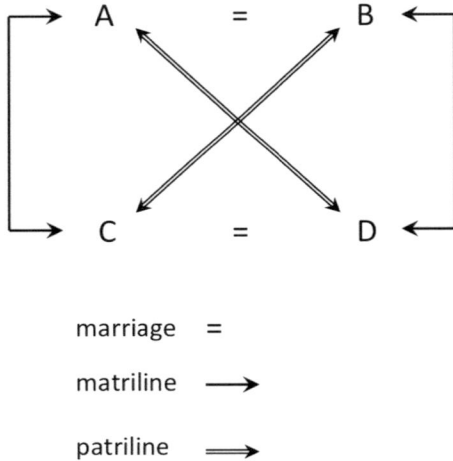

Figure 4.5: Sections (Northern Australia), from McConvell (1985: 32), after Radcliffe-Brown (1931).

McConvell also describes the doubly complex subsection systems. In a subsection system, the four categories of what used to be a section system are each divided in two (see McConvell for diagram and discussion). There are structural consequences. For example, a cross-cousin is a possible wife in a section system, but not in a subsection system.

These kinds of system are widespread in Aboriginal Australia. They are shared by groups that have completely different languages. Evans (2012) compares the situation to that of the modern system of military ranks as officially standardized by the Geneva Convention: groups in the same culture area have direct translations for the same offices in what is essentially the same system. In Northern Australia, a common cultural context has facilitated the widespread and stable status of particular types of kinship systems and vocabularies.

But there are many aspects of culture that seem less like systems and more like items. Eckert (2008) gives the example of a cut of jeans that happens to be fashionable among high school kids one year, though she urges us not to be tempted by the apparent individuability of such cultural elements. Something like the wearing of pegged pants or a way of pronouncing a vowel is always situated in an *indexical field*, as she puts it. When things like these are borrowed or adopted into new social settings they may be *segmented* out from a historical and indexical constellation of signs and meanings.

People who do this segmenting may be unaware of the larger (especially historical) connections. They will nevertheless give the item a place in a new system. Parry & Bloch (1989) make this point in connection with the historical adoption of money around the world: "in order to understand the way in which money is viewed it is vitally important to understand the cultural matrix into which it is incorporated" (Parry & Bloch 1989: 1).

Sahlins (1999) says that when new elements – everything from money to snowmobiles – are incorporated into cultural contexts, they are adopted for local purposes and given a "structural position" in "the cultural totality". Sahlins celebrates the appropriation by neotraditional people of elements from other people (and note we can distinguish between processes of appropriation that alter the item so as to make it fit into the receiving system versus those that alter the system so as to fit the incoming item; usually it is a combination of the two).

Sahlins is criticizing the idea that cultures like the Yupik become contaminated when people borrow modern innovations. His point is that once the items in question are borrowed, they are changed. They have new meanings in their new contexts.

4.5 Are cultural totalities illusory?

Consider the kinds of systems and relations of incorporation in language and culture just discussed. They show that we are never dealing with detached cultural items. But it does not follow from the striking systematicity of Australian sections and subsections that these ramp up into cultural totalities. It's possible that they do. After all, ethnographers have succeeded in writing reference descriptions of the knowledge, practices, values, and technologies of defined so-

4 The item/system problem

cial/cultural groups (Radcliffe-Brown 1922; Malinowski 1922; Firth 1936; Evans-Pritchard 1940; Fortes 1945). In the same way, linguists have succeeded in describing languages as totalities, not in the way a layperson might discretely label an imagined language – Dutch, Flemish, Thai, Lao, etc. – but rather in the technical sense of listing the full vocabulary and set of grammatical rules that any speaker in a community should know.

What is our evidence that such totalities exist? Both the "whole systems" and the "parts" of language seem clearly identifiable at first, but both ideas crumble upon close inspection (Le Page & Tabouret-Keller 1985; Hudson 1996). Any linguist knows that "a language" – in the sense of a community-wide system like French or Korean – is impossible to define by pointing at it: "as a totality it is inaccessible and indefinable; each of us has only partial experience of it" (Le Page & Tabouret-Keller 1985: 191).

"A language" in the sense that we normally mean it constitutes a system insofar as it is a set of interrelated items, such as words, each of which appears to be a stand-alone unit or element. The system idea is especially clear in the case of language for at least three reasons. First, the set of interrelated items in a language is a very large set. Second, we have strong intuitions about what is part of language and what is not. Third, this set contains numerous *sub*-systems. But still we never encounter a language as such, only fragments of languages, items like words and grammatical constructions, in contexts of speech and writing.

In their masterpiece on the nature of language, Le Page & Tabouret-Keller (1985: 8–9) challenge us to face the problem of "how to know when to speak of separate systems":

> If we start from the concept of an underlying system this becomes an extremely difficult, if not insoluble, problem; if however we approach it from the point of view of the degree of coherence evidenced in the behavior of a group of individuals, the problem is seen to be one of relationships and of stereotypes inherent in each individual.

Metalinguistic stances are real. But this does not mean that the systems those stances point to are real in the same way. How, then, can we have a clear causal account of linguistic systems? The answer – to bring us back to the item/system problem – is in the causality of social behavior at the micro level.

5 The micro/macro solution

Do cultural totalities exist? As members of a group we may feel certain that there is a cultural totality around us. But we never directly observe it. As Fortes (1949: 56) put it:

> Structure is not immediately visible in the "concrete reality". It is discovered by comparison, induction and analysis based on a sample of actual social happenings in which the institution, organization, usage etc. with which we are concerned appears in a variety of contexts. (Fortes 1949: 56)

This mode of discovery is not only used by ethnographers who are studying culture. It is also used by children whose task is to become competent adults (see Brown & Gaskins 2014).

If our experience of culture is in the micro, how do we extrapolate to the macro? When Parry & Bloch wrote about money and its status, they stressed that there are local differences between cultures and the effects on the meaning that money comes to have. But they also acknowledged a certain unity across cultures:

> [This unity is] neither in the meanings attributed to money nor in the moral evaluation of particular types of exchange, but rather in the way the totality of transactions form a general pattern which is part of the reproduction of social and ideological systems concerned with a time-scale far longer than the individual human life. (Parry & Bloch 1989: 1)

In terms that apply more generally to the micro/macro issue, there is "something very general about the relationship between the transient individual and the enduring social order which transcends the individual" (Parry & Bloch 1989: 2). It brings to mind Adam Smith's (1776: book 4, ch. 2) discussion of the relation between the motivations of individuals and the not-necessarily-intended community-level aggregate effects of their behavior (Schelling 1978; Hedström & Swedberg 1998; Rogers 2003). Parry & Bloch (1989: 29) contrast "short-term order" with "long-term reproduction", and they suggest that the two must be linked.

5 The micro/macro solution

This brings us back to the transmission criterion, an idea that will help to bridge the micro/macro divide. If a person is to function as a member of a social group, he or she needs to individually construct, in the ontogenetic frame, the ability to produce and properly interpret the normative behavior of others.

Not even a cultural totality is exempt from the transmission criterion. Individual people have to learn the component parts of a totality during their lifetimes (in ontogeny), and they must be motivated to reproduce the behaviors (in microgeny and enchrony) that stabilize the totality and cause it to endure beyond their own lives and lifetimes (in diachrony). A person's motivation can be in the form of a salient external pressure such as the threat of state violence. But it usually comes from the less visible force of normative accountability (Heritage 1984; Enfield 2013).

In the social/cultural contexts of our daily lives, everything we do will be interpreted as meaningful. "The big question is not whether actors understand each other or not", wrote Garfinkel (1952: 367). "The fact is that they do understand each other, that they *will* understand each other, but the catch is that they will understand each other regardless of how they *would* be understood." This means that if you are a member of a social group, you are not exempt from having others take your actions to have meanings, whether or not these were the meanings you wanted your actions to have.

As Levinson (1983: 321) phrases it, also echoing Goffman and Sacks, we are "not so much constrained by rules or sanctions, as caught up in a web of inferences'. We will be held to account for others" interpretations of our behavior and we know this whether we like it or not.[1] This is a powerful force in getting us to conform. Accountability to norms "constitutes the foundation of socially organized conduct as a self-producing environment of 'perceivedly normal' activities" (Heritage 1984: 119). The thing that tells us what counts as normal is of course the culture.

> With respect to the production of normatively appropriate conduct, all that is required is that the actors have, and attribute to one another, a reflexive awareness of the normative accountability of their actions. For actors who, under these conditions, calculate the consequences of their actions in reflexively transforming the circumstances and relationships in which they find themselves, will routinely find that their interests are well served by

---

[1] This does not mean that we are accountable for just any interpretation, but only those interpretations that are grounded in social norms. For example, if you are in the habit of going barefoot on the street, you can expect people to draw attention to this whether you like it or not (in a way that they will not if you are in the habit of wearing shoes).

normatively appropriate conduct. With respect to the anarchy of interests, the choice is not between normatively organized co-operative conduct and the disorganized pursuit of interests. Rather, normative accountability is the "grid" by reference to which *whatever* is done will become visible and assessable. (Heritage 1984: 117)

One might ask what is "normatively appropriate conduct". The answer must include any of the kinds of behaviors discussed in the above section on cultural systems: for example, behaving in accordance with the rules of a section system by marrying someone of the right category (or being able to give reasons why you have done otherwise). They would not be cultural behaviors if they were not regimented in a community by accountability to norms (and probably also laws).

So the path that is both the least resistant and the most empowering for a person is to learn the system that generates a shared set of normative interpretations of people's behavior, and then go with the flow. This is how the totality cannot exist without the individuals, while – paradoxically – appearing to do just that. We create and maintain the very systems that constrain us.

The close relationship between short-term order and long-term reproduction is an asymmetrical one. Short-term order is where the causal locus of transmission is found. It is where acceleration, deceleration, and transformation in cultural transmission occurs (Schelling 1978; Sperber 1985, 1996; Rogers 2003).

From all of this it is clear that cultural systems exist and they both constrain us and guide us. The question is: How are systems transmitted? The regulation of individual behavior in the cultural totality is not achieved by mere emergence. It is not like the self-oriented behavior of a bird in the seemingly concerted movement of a flock. Individuals' behavior is regulated by norms, in an effectively telic way. A good deal of cultural regimentation is done through explicit instruction, often with reference to norms, and sometimes with reference to punishable laws.

To see how whole cultural systems are transmitted, we have to draw on item-based processes of transmission. As we saw in the last chapter, the only good causal account we have for social transmission through populations and across generations is one that works in terms of items, not whole systems.

5.1 The combinatoric nature of cultural items in general

Recall that the context bias is grounded in the fact that one cannot behold any so-called item without beholding it *in relation to* something else, including not only

5 The micro/macro solution

things of similar kinds, but also the social norms and intentions associated with items and the contexts in which they appear. So, I cannot know what a hammer is if I do not see it in relation to the human body, timber and nails, people's intentions to build things, conventional techniques for construction, and so on.

These relations – which themselves are interrelated – form an indispensible part of what I am referring to by the term *item*. When a cultural item diffuses, what is diffusing is something less like an object and more like a combinatoric relation. So, a hammer incorporates a handle or grip. The handle or grip has a combinatoric relation to the human hand insofar as the handle and the hand are practically and normatively designed to go together. The handle is designed that way because of how the human hand is. The handle only makes sense in terms of a person's hand.

This going together of the handle and the human hand is like a grammatical rule. In a similar way, the handle of the hammer and the *head* of the hammer go together both practically and normatively. The head of the hammer, in turn, goes with a nail. The nail, in turn, goes with timber, and so forth. So we see how the cultural items that diffuse in communities necessarily incorporate – and advertize – their rules of fit with other items.

The sprawling yet structured systems that we call languages have the same kinds of properties of incorporation and contextualization that I have just described for concrete objects. So, if speakers of a language have borrowed a word from another language, this does not mean they have merely adopted a pairing of sound and concept. They must also have adopted a way of relating the word to their existing language system (whether or not this relation resembles the one used in the source system).

The word will not be usable if it does not have combinatoric properties that specify how it fits with other words. The norms for combining the word in usage may be borrowed along with the word itself, or they may be provided by existing structures in the borrowing language, or they may even be innovated in the process of incorporation.

The combinatoric relations surrounding a cultural item do not have to diffuse along with that item. But a cultural element must have *some* combinatoric relation to other cultural items in the same domain if it is to function and circulate. That relation can just as well be invented by the people who adopt the item, in line with the contraints of their own culture and world view. This is the point that authors like Sahlins and Eckert, mentioned above, have stressed for culture.

So, structuralist linguists like Donegan & Stampe (1983: 1) are right when they say that a language "is not just a collection of autonomous parts". But this does not mean that a language is "a self-contained whole". The same applies when cultural anthropologists refer to the "cultural totality".

We never encounter whole systems except one fragment at a time, in microgeny and enchrony. Our "partial experience" (Le Page & Tabouret-Keller 1985: 191) is not experience of the whole system. But nor is it experience of stand-alone items. When we experience culture, we experience meaningful items in relations of functional incorporation and contextualization with other such items.

Each such relation is, effectively, a combinatoric principle, like a norm for forming a grammatical sentence or for using a hammer and nail in the appropriate way. These relations are at the center of the framework being proposed here. These relations are what is transmitted. They have an inherent connection to a cultural system or field, but this system or field has no pre-given size or outer borderline.

Bloch (2000) says that old critiques of diffusionism in anthropology also work as critiques of today's item-based accounts. I would say that the problems are handled by the simple conceptual shift being proposed here. The relevant unit of cultural transmission (meme or whatever) is not *a piece*. The relevant unit is *a piece and its functional relation to a context*. This might seem obvious. But when we make it explicit, the fear of a disembodied view of cultural units goes away. The required conceptual move is not to take items and put them in a context. Their relation to a context is what *defines* them.

5.2 Solving the item/system problem in language

Identifying the *relation to context* as the common unit of analysis of both items and systems is necessary but not yet sufficient. We need an account of how this scales up into large structured sets of such relations. Let us consider the question in connection to language. Every linguistic convention in a community is a product of general mechanisms of social diffusion. Each convention has its own history. Every word, every morpheme, every construction has followed its own historical path to community-level acceptance. As Bloomfield (1933: 444) said, "individual forms may have had very different adventures".

This does not mean languages are mere bundles of items. They are large, structured, systematic wholes. Psychologically, languages exist in people's minds and bodies. They take the form of idiolects. Intersubjectively, languages exist at a *community* level to the extent that people's idiolects are effectively alike in structure and content, as demonstrated by the evidently tolerable degree of success of communication (Enfield 2015). We can now specify some forces that bring items together and structure them into systems.

5.3 Centripetal and systematizing forces

When we say that two people speak the same language, we mean that two individuals' knowledge of a language system – synchronically, as can be seen in their enchronic and microgenetic behavior – is effectively (though never exactly) shared. This sharedness exists because a large number of the same linguistic variants have been channelled, in a huge set, along the same historical pathways. This gives the impression that a language is passed down as a whole, transcending lifetime after lifetime of the individuals who learn and embody the system.

This is the point made by Thomason & Kaufman (1988): Normal social conditions enable children, as first language learners, to construct idiolects that effectively match the idiolects of the people they learn from – i.e., those with whom children share a household and an immediate social environment, and who are, incidentally, most likely to share their genes. Normal transmission is what allows historical linguists to abstract from the fact that each linguistic variant has its own career, and in turn to treat the whole language as having one spatial-historical trajectory.

In many cases this is a reasonable and successful methodological presumption (Haspelmath 2004). But in situations other than those of normal transmission (Le Page & Tabouret-Keller 1985; Thomason & Kaufman 1988), linguistic items do not always travel together, but may follow separate paths, making visible what is always true but usually obscured by items' common destiny in practice, namely: Each item has its own history.

Genealogical continuity in language change is typically taken to be the norm. Whenever we see that linguistic systems are permeable, for instance in certain language contact situations where the components of languages are prised apart, special explanations are demanded.

5.4 On normal transmission

To say that a child inherits a language from her parents is a misleading representation of what happens in language acquisition. The idiolect of the child is not acquired like DNA in a bundle. Patterns of constituency and grammatical relations do not unfold in children like the shapes of their bodily organs. Through practice, children have to learn, construct, and maintain skills and ideas for ways of saying things.

> The "rules" of a child's "native language" … are in any case likely to be tentative hypotheses, easily modified by fresh semantic needs, fresh contacts,

5.4 On normal transmission

fresh analogies. "Syntax" in the grammarian's sense is what emerges from this process, not what it starts from. (Le Page & Tabouret-Keller 1985: 190)

Logic and universal grammar, then, are targets towards which, rather than the starting point from which, human linguistic activity proceeds. The origins of that activity are like those of a game which gradually develops among players, each of whom can experiment with changes of the rules, all of whom are umpires judging whether new rules are acceptable. (Le Page & Tabouret-Keller 1985: 197)

This transmission takes place through air, over days, weeks, months, years, with interference and noise. Every bit of the idiolect's structure has to be passed over and constructed from scratch by the learner. This task is made possible by the sheer deluge of linguistic data – a *Niagara of words*, as Hayakawa (1978: 12) called it – which people are exposed to, and produce in turn. Child language acquisition is a process of building (Tomasello 2003), resulting in something like a grammatical totality in the child's competence. But whatever totality a person has built, it is instantiated somehow in the head and so (a) will never go public as a whole and (b) will be destroyed when the person dies. The system is neither observed nor passed on as a whole unit, only ever fragment-by-fragment.

Dunbar (1996) has hypothesized that prelinguistic human ancestors created language as a way to lessen time pressure due to the need to manage an expanding number of social associates. Sustaining a social network by means of linguistic contact is time-consuming. Where personal exchange or strong network ties are involved, we are necessarily oriented towards a limited group. The size of networks is constrained by the time it takes to maintain these relationships. However, the number of non-personal exposure ties – passive seeing and hearing, especially due to media and high population density – is potentially massive. The invention of writing has drastically changed the proportion of personal and non-personal sources of exposure to innovation.

Thomason & Kaufman (1988) invoke an idea of *normal transmission* (see above). They define normal transmission "by exclusion" (Thomason & Kaufman 1988: 10), in terms of how "perfectly" all sub-systems of a language are reproduced in children's idiolects. In normal transmission, linguistic input from outgroup people has negligible impact on a child's construction of an idiolect highly convergent with the idiolects of the parents' generation. Normal transmission, in Thomason and Kaufman's sense, is a social fact (Thomason & Kaufman 1988: 12), though it is defined by formal facts about child language acquisition in a community:

5 *The micro/macro solution*

> [A] claim of genetic relationship [between a "parent" and a "daughter" language] entails systematic correspondences in all parts of the language because that is what results from normal transmission: what is transmitted is an entire language – that is, a complex set of interrelated lexical, phonological, morphosyntactic, and semantic structures. (Thomason & Kaufman 1988: 11)

Here is how I understand Thomason and Kaufman's point. To say that a "genetic" relationship holds between parent and daughter languages is to use a metaphor, and to use this metaphor is harmless as long as the older generation's idiolects are reproduced so closely in the idiolects of the younger generation that it is *as if* the new idiolects were replicas of the old. This is effectively what happens in the case of normal transmission. There is a relentless and focussed linguistic sign deluge from people of the learner's own group.

But another question remains. How can we explain the relative impermeability of linguistic systems in circumstances of normal transmission? Stability in conventional systems is no less in need of explanation than variation or change (Bourdieu 1977; Sperber 1996; Sperber & Hirschfeld 2004). What are the forces that cause linguistic variants to follow en masse a single path of diffusion and circulation, and to hold together as structured systems? Let us briefly consider three such forces.

5.4.1 Sociometric closure

A first centripetal force is sociometric closure. This arises from a trade-off between strength and number of relationship ties in a social network. If a person is going to maintain a social relationship, she has to commit a certain amount of time to this. Time is a finite resource. This puts a structural constraint on the possible number of relationships one can maintain (Hill & Dunbar 2003). The result is a relatively closed circulation of currency within a social economy of linguistic items. It causes people's inventories of items (i.e., their vocabularies, etc.) to overlap significantly, or to be effectively identical, within social networks.

This helps to account for how people who interact often can have a common set of variants. It does not account for the system-like nature of the relations among those items. We turn now to two forces of systematization inherent to grammar, in the paradigmatic and syntagmatic axes.

5.4.2 Trade-off effects

One systematizing force comes from functional trade-off effects that arise when a goal-oriented person has alternative means to similar ends. When different items come to be used in a single functional domain, those items can become formally and structurally affected by their relative status in the set. This happens because the items compete for a single resource, namely, our selection of them as means for our communicative ends.

When Zipf (1949) undertook "a study of human speech as a set of tools", he compared the words of a language with the tools in an artisan's workshop. Different items have different functions, and different relative functional loads. In a vocabulary, Zipf (1949: 21) argued, there is an internal economy of words, with trade-offs that result in system effects like the observed correlation between the length of a word (relative to other words) and the frequency of use of the word (relative to that of other words).

Zipf reasoned that "the more frequent tools will tend to be the lighter, smaller, older, more versatile tools, and also the tools that are more thoroughly integrated with the action of other tools" (Zipf 1949: 73). He showed that the more we regard a set of available means as alternatives to each other in a functional domain, the more they become defined in terms of each other, acquiring new characteristics as a result of their role in the economy they operate in. In other words: The more we treat a set of items as a system, the more it becomes a system.

5.4.3 Item-utterance fit, aka content-frame fit

A final key source of grammatical structure is grammatical structure itself. The *utterance* is a core structural locus in language. An utterance is a local context for the interpretation of a linguistic item. It is an essential ratchet between item and system. As Kirby writes, although "semantic information" is what linguistic utterances most obviously convey, "there is another kind of information that can be conveyed by any linguistic production, and that is information about the linguistic system itself".

> When I produce the sentence "these berries are good" I may be propagating cultural information about the edibility of items in the environment via the content of the sentence. At the same time I may also be propagating information about the construction of sentences in my language. (Kirby 2013: 123)

5 The micro/macro solution

In this way, an utterance is a frame and a vehicle for replicating linguistic variants (Croft 2000).

Item-utterance fit is the structural fit between diffusible types of linguistic items and the token utterances in which they appear. It is an instance of the more general *content-frame* schema (Levelt 1989) also observed in phonology (MacNeilage 1998; see Enfield 2013: 54–55), and a case of the "functional relation to context" defined above as a common property of items and systems. Now we see that it is not just a common property. It is the very property that connects items with systems. An utterance is an incorporating and contextualizing frame for the diffusion of replicable linguistic items, *and* it is a frame for the diffusion of the combinatoric rules from which the higher-level system is built.

5.5 A solution to the item/system problem?

The above considerations suggest that the item/system problem can be solved if the following three forces apply in the biased transmission of cultural items:

1. *Congregation:* Items are brought together and "bundled" by the population-level effects of inward-directed sociometric biases.

2. *Specialization:* Items then effectively compete for selection in the same functional contexts, and come to be specialized as alternative means for related functional ends.

3. *Combination:* Items in a set come to combine with each other in functional ways, via context biases and the relation of item-utterance fit.

We can expect there to be analogous relations to item-utterance fit (=content-frame fit) in the domain of culture. Think, for instance, of systems of social relations in kinship, or systems of material culture and technology in households and villages.

Zipf's (1949) analogy is useful here. For his "economy of tools-for-jobs and jobs-for-tools" to get off the ground, one first needs a *workshop,* somewhere the set of tools is assembled in one place, and made accessible to a person with goals. In language and culture, this is achieved by sociometric closure (§ 5.4.1, above): the more you talk with certain people, the more ways of talking you will share with these people. Then, one works with the set of tools, using them as alternative specialized means to similar or related ends (§ 5.4.2, above). Finally, these tools will, whether by design or by nature, enter into the relations of incorporation

5.5 A solution to the item/system problem?

and contextualization that define their both their functional potential and their system status (§ 5.4.3, above).

Now this should look familiar to the linguist. Once we get an *inventory* or lexicon of items that have specalized functions within a given domain, they will naturally enter into the *paradigmatic* and *syntagmatic* relations that define semiotic systems in the classical sense.

6 Conclusion

Ever since Darwin's earliest remarks on the uncanny similarity between language change and natural history in biology, there has been a persistent conceptual unclarity in evolutionary approaches to cultural change. This unclarity concerns the units of analysis.

In some cases the unit is said to be the language system as a whole. A language, then, is "like a species" (Darwin 1871: 60; cf. Mufwene 2001: 192–194). If so, then we are talking about a population of idiolects that is coterminous with a population of bodies (allowing, of course, that in the typical situation – multilingualism – one body houses more than one linguistic system).

On another view, the unit of analysis is any unit that forms *part* of a language, such as a word or a piece of grammar. "A struggle for life is constantly going on amongst the words and grammatical forms in each language" (Müller 1870, cited in Darwin 1871: 60). By contrast with the idea of populations of idiolects, this suggests that there are populations *of items* (akin to Zipf's economy of word-tools), where these items are produced, and perceived, in the context of spoken utterances.

While some of us instinctively think first in terms of items, and others of us first in terms of systems, we do not have the luxury of ignoring either. Neither an item nor a system can exist without the other. The challenge is to characterize the relation between the two. This relation is the one thing that defines them both.

The issue is not just the relative status of items and systems but the causal relations between them. If the distinction between item and system is a matter of framing, it is no less consequential for that. We not only have to define the differences between item phenomena and system phenomena, we must know which ones we are talking about and when. And we must show whether, and if so how, we can translate statements about one into statements about the other.

6 Conclusion

6.1 Natural causes of language

"We might gain considerable insight into the mainsprings of human behavior", wrote Zipf (1949: v), "if we viewed it purely as a natural phenomenon like everything else in the universe". This does not mean that we cannot embrace the anthropocentrism, subjectivity, and self-reflexivity of human affairs. It does mean that underneath all of that, our analyses remain accountable to natural, causal claims. In this book we have developed a causally explicit model for the transmission of cultural items, and we have approached a solution to the item/system problem that builds solely on these item-based biases. I submit that the biases required for item evolution – never forgetting that "item" here really means "something-and-its-functional-relation-to-a-context" – are sufficient not only to account for how and why certain cultural items win or lose. They also account for the key relational forces that link items with systems.

We have confronted the item/system problem. To solve it, we reached for the most tangible known causal mechanism for the existence of linguistic and cultural reality: item-based transmission. The outcome is this. With the right definition of "item" – as always having a functional relation to context – we can have an item-based account for linguistic and cultural reality that gives us a system ontology for free.

6.2 Toward a framework

Why do neighboring languages share structures in common? In earlier work on language contact, maintenance, and change (Enfield 2003, 2005, 2008, 2011), I considered some of the challenges that this question raises. This led me to confront the conceptual problems I have discussed in this book. They are problems of causality. What makes languages the way they are? What causes a language to have certain features and not others? How permeable are language systems? These questions led me to look for a causal account of the ontology of language. I have tried in the above chapters to present some of the ideas that came out. Together, these ideas suggest a natural, causal framework for understanding the foundations of language. The framework has two conceptual components:

> *Causal frames*: There are multiple frames or "time-scales" within which change in linguistic and other cultural systems can be causally effected. While most approaches work within just one or two of these frames, all of these frames should be considered together, with special attention to

the links between them. As explicated in Chapter 2, the framework recognizes six such frames, under the rubric of MOPEDS: *microgenetic*, invoking cognitive and motoric processes for producing and comprehending language and other goal-directed behavior; *ontogenetic*, invoking lifespan processes by which people, usually as children, acquire linguistic and cultural knowledge and skills; *phylogenetic*, invoking ways in which the requisite cognitive capacities have evolved in our species; *enchronic*, invoking the sequential interlocking of social actions in linguistic clothing; *diachronic*, invoking historical change, conducted socially in human populations; and *synchronic*, any approach, such as linguistic or ethnographic description, that does not explicitly invoke notions of process.

Transmission biases: A socially- and cognitively-grounded account of the genesis, diffusion, and conventionalization of innovations in human populations must provide a causal basis for how it is that social conventions – such as the linguistic and ethnographic facts that we observe – are the way they are. As explicated in Chapter 3, the causal machinery for diffusion of types of behavior (including language) within a population is a driving force – an engine of sorts – with four linked loci: *exposure* to a bit of behavior, *representation* of that bit of behavior, subsequent *reproduction* of that bit of behavior, and *material* instantiation of some trace of the behavior (leading to exposure of others, feeding back into the process anew). Each locus is a site where the chain of diffusion may be broken, reinforced, or transformed: Such breaks, reinforcements, and transformations come from *biases* that may operate on each locus (Chapter 3 gives the details). There are many of these biases. Some are cognitive. For example, if a linguistic construction is easier to learn, it will diffuse better. Some are social. For example, if more prestigious people model an innovation, other people are more likely to copy it.

These two conceptual pillars of a framework for understanding the natural causes of language should be enough to provide the raw materials for explaining the ontology of linguistic systems.

Linguistic system ontology is a puzzle because items (in contexts) are the only things that circulate and yet somehow systems exist. If our conceptual framework recognizes multiple coexisting causal frames and multiple coexisting loci of transmission, it becomes possible to see how gaps and interfaces between these frames and loci provide the traction for system emergence. At least it becomes possible to study the problem. Empirical and theoretical investigations

6 Conclusion

will have to draw not only on the linguistics of descriptive grammar, semantics, pragmatics, and typology, but also on sociological research on innovation diffusion, sociolinguistic research on social networks, and the natural science of cultural evolution. A framework like this should allow us to be maximally explicit about the causal processes that create linguistic and other cultural facts.

Bibliography

Aikhenvald, Alexandra Y. & R. M. W. Dixon. 1998. Dependencies between grammatical systems. *Language* 74(1). 56–80.

Atkinson, J. Maxwell & John Heritage. 1984. *Structures of social action: Studies in conversation analysis*. Cambridge: Cambridge University Press.

Aureli, Filippo, Colleen M. Schaffner, Christophe Boesch, Simon K. Bearder, Josep Call, Colin A. Chapman, Richard Connor, Anthony Di Fiore, Robin I. M. Dunbar, S. Peter Henzi, Kay Holekamp, Amanda H. Korstjens, Robert Layton, Phyllis Lee, Julia Lehmann, Joseph H. Manson, Gabriel Ramos-Fernandez, Karen B. Strier & Carel P. van Schaaik. 2008. Fission-fusion dynamics. *Current Anthropology* 49(4). 627–654.

Baddeley, Alan D. 1986. *Working memory*. Oxford: Clarendon Press.

Bakhtin, Mikhail M. 1981. *The dialogic imagination*. Austin/London: University of Texas Press.

Bickel, Balthasar. 2014. Linguistic diversity and universals. In N. J. Enfield, Paul Kockelman & Jack Sidnell (eds.), *The Cambridge handbook of linguistic anthropology*, 102–127. Cambridge: Cambridge University Press.

Bloch, Maurice. 2000. A well-disposed social anthropologist's problems with memes. In Robert Aunger (ed.), *Darwinizing culture: The status of memetics as a science*, Oxford: Oxford University Press.

Bloomfield, Leonard. 1933. *Language*. New York: Holt.

Boto, Luis. 2010. Horizontal gene transfer in evolution: Facts and challenges. *Proceedings of the Royal Society B: Biological Sciences* 277(1683). 819–827.

Bourdieu, Pierre. 1977. *Outline of a theory of practice*. Cambridge: Cambridge University Press.

Boyd, Robert & Peter J. Richerson. 1985. *Culture and the evolutionary process*. Chicago: University of Chicago Press.

Boyd, Robert & Peter J. Richerson. 2005. *The origin and evolution of cultures*. New York: Oxford University Press.

6 Bibliography

Brown, Penelope & Suzanne Gaskins. 2014. Language acquisition and language socialization. In N. J. Enfield, Paul Kockelman & Jack Sidnell (eds.), *The Cambridge handbook of linguistic anthropology*, 187–226. Cambridge: Cambridge University Press.

Bybee, Joan. 2010. *Language, usage and cognition*. Cambridge: Cambridge University Press.

Chafe, Wallace. 2000. Loci of diversity and convergence in thought and language. In Martin Pütz & Marjolijn Verspoor (eds.), *Explorations in linguistic relativity*, 101–123. Amsterdam: Benjamins.

Chater, Nick & Morten H. Christiansen. 2010. Language acquisition meets language evolution. *Cognitive Science* 34(7). 1131–57.

Christiansen, Morten H. & Nick Chater. 2008. Language as shaped by the brain. *Behavioral and Brain Sciences* 31(5). 489–509.

Clark, Eve V. 2009. *First language acquisition*. Cambridge: Cambridge University Press.

Clark, Herbert H. & Barbara C. Malt. 1984. Psychological constraints on language: A commentary on Bresnan and Kaplan and on Givón. In Walter Kintsch, James R. Miller & Peter G. Polson (eds.), *Methods and tactics in cognitive science*, 191–214. Hillsdale, NJ: Lawrence Erlbaum.

Cole, Michael. 1996. *Cultural psychology: A once and future discipline*. Harvard: Harvard University Press.

Cole, Michael. 2007. Phylogeny and cultural history in ontogeny. *Journal of Physiology, Paris* 101(4). 236–246.

Cowley, Stephen J. 2011. *Distributed language*. Amsterdam: John Benjamins.

Croft, William. 2000. *Explaining language change: an evolutionary approach*. Harlow: Longman.

Curnow, Timothy Jowan. 2001. What language features can be 'borrowed'? In Alexandra Y. Aikhenvald & R. M. W. Dixon (eds.), *Areal diffusion and genetic inheritance: problems in comparative linguistics*, 412–436. Oxford: Oxford University Press.

Cutler, Anne. 2012. *Native listening: Language experience and the recognition of spoken words*. Cambridge, MA: MIT Press.

Darwin, Charles. 1859. *On the origin of species by means of natural selection*. London: John Murray.

Darwin, Charles. 1871. *The descent of man, and selection in relation to sex*. London: John Murray.

Darwin, Charles. 1872. *The expression of the emotions in man and animals*. London: John Murray.

Davidson, Donald. 2006. *The essential Davidson*. Oxford: Clarendon.
Dawkins, Richard. 1976. *The selfish gene*. Oxford: Oxford University Press.
Dawkins, Richard. 1982. *The extended phenotype: The long reach of the gene*. Oxford: Oxford University Press.
Dawkins, Richard. 1999. Foreword. In Susan Blakemore, *The meme machine*, vii–xvii. Oxford: Oxford University Press.
Dingemanse, Mark, Francisco Torreira & N. J. Enfield. 2013. Is "huh?" a universal word? Conversational infrastructure and the convergent evolution of linguistic items. *PLOS One* 8(11). e78273.
Dixon, R. M. W. 1997. *The rise and fall of languages*. Cambridge: Cambridge University Press.
Dixon, R. M. W. 2010. *Basic linguistic theory*. Oxford: Oxford University Press.
Dixon, R. M. W. 2014. Basics of a language. In N. J. Enfield, Paul Kockelman & Jack Sidnell (eds.), *The Cambridge handbook of linguistic anthropology*, 29–47. Cambridge: Cambridge University Press.
Donald, Merlin. 2007. The slow process: A hypothetical cognitive adaptation for distributed cognitive networks. *Journal of Physiology, Paris* 101(4-6). 214–222.
Donegan, Jane & David Stampe. 1983. Rhythm and the holistic organization of language structure. In John F. Richardson, Mitchell Marks & Amy Chukerman (eds.), *The interplay of phonology, morphology, and syntax*, 337–353. Chicago: Chicago Linguistic Society.
Donegan, Jane & David Stampe. 2002. South-east Asian features in the Munda languages: Evidence for the analytic-to-synthetic drift of Munda. *Proceedings of the 28th Annual Meeting of the Berkeley Linguistics Society, Special Session on Tibeto-Burman and Southeast Asian Linguistics, in Honor of Prof. James A. Matisoff* 111–129.
Dor, Daniel, Chris Knight & Jerome Lewis (eds.). 2014. *The social origins of language: Studies in the evolution of language*. Oxford: Oxford University Press.
Dunbar, Robin I. M. 1996. *Grooming, gossip and the evolution of language*. London: Faber and Faber.
Durkheim, Emile. 1912. *The elementary forms of the religious life*. Oxford: Oxford University Press.
Eckert, Penelope. 2000. *Linguistic variation as social practice*. Oxford: Blackwell.
Eckert, Penelope. 2008. Variation and the indexical field. *Journal of Sociolinguistics* 12(4). 453–476.
Enfield, N. J. 2002. *Ethnosyntax: explorations in culture and grammar*. Oxford: Oxford University Press.

6 Bibliography

Enfield, N. J. 2003. *Linguistic epidemiology: Semantics and grammar of language contact in mainland Southeast Asia.* London: Routledge Curzon.

Enfield, N. J. 2005. Areal linguistics and mainland Southeast Asia. *Annual Review of Anthropology* 34. 181–206.

Enfield, N. J. 2007. *A grammar of Lao* (Mouton Grammar Library 38). Berlin: Mouton de Gruyter.

Enfield, N. J. 2008. Transmission biases in linguistic epidemiology. *Journal of Language Contact* 2. 295–306.

Enfield, N. J. 2009. *The anatomy of meaning: Speech, gesture, and composite utterances.* Cambridge: Cambridge University Press.

Enfield, N. J. 2011. Linguistic diversity in mainland Southeast Asia. In N. J. Enfield (ed.), *Dynamics of human diversity: The case of mainland Southeast Asia*, 63–80. Canberra: Pacific Linguistics.

Enfield, N. J. 2013. *Relationship thinking: Agency, enchrony, and human sociality.* New York: Oxford University Press.

Enfield, N. J. 2015. *The utility of meaning: What words mean and why.* Oxford: Oxford University Press.

Enfield, N. J., Paul Kockelman & Jack Sidnell (eds.). 2014. *The cambridge handbook of linguistic anthropology.* Cambridge: CUP.

Enfield, N. J. & Stephen C. Levinson. 2006. *Roots of human sociality: Culture, cognition, and interaction.* London: Berg.

Enfield, N. J. & Jack Sidnell. 2014. Language presupposes an enchronic infrastructure for social interaction. In Daniel Dor, Chris Knight & Jerome Lewis (eds.), *The social origins of language: Studies in the evolution of language*, 92–104. Oxford: Oxford University Press.

Evans, Nicholas D. 2012. An enigma under an enigma: Unsolved linguistic paradoxes in a sometime continent of hunter-gatherers. Conference presentation, Amsterdam 2012.

Evans-Pritchard, E. E. 1940. *The Nuer: A description of the modes of livelihood and political institutions of a Nilotic people.* Oxford: Clarendon Press.

Everett, Daniel L. 2005. Cultural constraints on grammar and cognition in Pirahã. *Current Anthropology* 46(4). 621–646.

Everett, Daniel L. 2012. *Language: The cultural tool.* London: Profile.

Fillmore, Charles J. 1982. Frame semantics. In Linguistic Society of Korea (ed.), *Linguistics in the morning calm*, 111–137. Seoul: Hanshin.

Firth, Raymond. 1936. *We the Tikopia: A sociological study of kinship in primitive Polynesia.* London: Routledge.

Fodor, Jerry A. 1987. *Psychosemantics.* Cambridge, MA: MIT Press.

Fortes, Meyer. 1945. *The dynamics of clanship among the Tallensi.* Oxford: Oxford University Press.

Fortes, Meyer. 1949. *Social structure.* Oxford: Clarendon Press.

Fortes, Meyer & E. E. Evans-Pritchard (eds.). 1940. *African political systems.* Oxford: Oxford University Press.

von der Gabelentz, Georg. 1891. *Die Sprachwissenschaft, ihre Aufgaben, Methoden und bisherigen Ergebnisse.* London: Routledge/Thoemmes Press. 2nd edn.

Garfinkel, Harold. 1952. *The perception of the other: A study in social order.* Harvard: Harvard University Press.

Garfinkel, Harold. 1967. *Studies in ethnomethodology.* New Jersey: Prentice-Hall.

Gergely, György & Gergely Csibra. 2006. Sylvia's recipe: The role of imitation and pedagogy in the transmission of cultural knowledge. In N. J. Enfield & Stephen C. Levinson (eds.), *Roots of human sociality: culture, cognition, and interaction*, 229–255. London: Berg.

Gibson, James J. 1979. *The ecological approach to visual perception.* Boston: Houghton Mifflin.

Gigerenzer, Gerd, Ralph Hertwig & Thorsten Pachur (eds.). 2011. *Heuristics: The foundations of adaptive behavior.* New York: Oxford University Press.

Givón, Talmy. 1984. *Syntax: a functional-typological introduction.* Amsterdam: John Benjamins.

Gladwell, Malcolm. 2000. *The tipping point: How little things can make a big difference.* Boston: Little and Brown.

Gould, Stephen Jay. 1977. *Ontogeny and phylogeny.* Harvard: Harvard University Press.

Granovetter, Mark. 1973. The strength of weak ties. *American Journal of Sociology* 78. 1360–1380.

Greenberg, Joseph H. 1966. Some universals of grammar with particular reference to the order of meaningful elements. In Joseph H. Greenberg (ed.), *Universals of language (second edition)*, 73–113. Cambridge, MA: MIT Press.

Grice, H. Paul. 1975. Logic and conversation. In Peter Cole & Jerry L. Morgan (eds.), *Speech acts*, 41–58. New York: Academic Press.

Hale, Kenneth L. 1986. Notes on world view and semantic categories: Some Warlpiri examples. In Pieter Muysken & Henk van Riemsdijk (eds.), *Features and projections*, 233–254. Dordrecht: Foris.

Harris, Alice C. & Lyle Campbell. 1995. *Historical syntax in cross-linguistic perspective.* Cambridge: Cambridge University Press.

Haspelmath, Martin. 2004. How hopeless is genealogical linguistics, and how advanced is areal linguistics? *Studies in Language* 28(1). 209–223.

6 Bibliography

Haspelmath, Martin. 2007. Pre-established categories don't exist: consequences for language description and typology. *Linguistic typology* 11(1). 119–132.

Hayakawa, Samuel Ichiye. 1978. *Language in thought and action.* San Diego: Harcourt Brace Jovanovich. Enlarged edition.

Hedström, Peter & Richard Swedberg. 1998. *Social mechanisms: an analytical approach to social theory.* Cambridge: Cambridge University Press.

Heritage, John. 1984. *Garfinkel and ethnomethodology.* Cambridge: Polity Press.

Herrmann, Esther, Josep Call, María Victoria Hernández-Lloreda, Brian Hare & Michael Tomasello. 2007. Humans have evolved specialized skills of social cognition: The cultural intelligence hypothesis. *Science* 317. 1360–1366.

Hill, R. A. & Robin I. M. Dunbar. 2003. Social network size in humans. *Human Nature* 14. 53–72.

Hockett, Charles F. 1987. *Refurbishing our foundations: Elementary linguistics from an advanced point of view.* Amsterdam: John Benjamins.

Hopper, Paul J. & Elizabeth Closs Traugott. 1993. *Grammaticalization.* Cambridge: Cambridge University Press.

Hudson, R. A. 1996. *Sociolinguistics (second edition).* Cambridge: Cambridge University Press.

Hurford, James R. 2007. *The origins of meaning.* Oxford: Oxford University Press.

Hurford, James R. 2012. *The origins of grammar.* Oxford: Oxford University Press.

Jacob, François. 1977. Evolution and tinkering. *Science* (196). 1161–1966.

Kandel, Eric R. 2009. The biology of memory: A forty-year perspective. *The Journal of Neuroscience* 29(41). 12748–12756.

Keller, Rudi. 1994. *On language change: The invisible hand in language.* London: Routledge.

Kirby, Simon. 1999. *Function, selection, and innateness: The emergence of language universals.* Oxford: Oxford University Press.

Kirby, Simon. 2013. Transitions: The evolution of linguistic replicators. In *The language phenomenon*, 121–138. Berlin, Heidelberg: Springer Verlag.

Kirby, Simon, Hannah Cornish & Kenny Smith. 2008. Cumulative cultural evolution in the laboratory: an experimental approach to the origins of structure in human language. *Proceedings of the National Academy of Sciences of America* 105(31). 10681–10686.

Kirby, Simon, Kenny Smith & Henry Brighton. 2004. From UG to universals: Linguistic adaptation through iterated learning. *Studies in Language* 28(3). 587–607.

Klein, Wolfgang. 1986. *Second language acquisition.* Cambridge: Cambridge University Press.

Kockelman, Paul. 2005. The semiotic stance. *Semiotica* 157(1/4). 233–304.

Kockelman, Paul. 2006. Residence in the world: Affordances, instruments, actions, roles, and identities. *Semiotica* 162(1-4). 19–71.

Kockelman, Paul. 2013. *Agent, person, subject, self: A theory of ontology, interaction, and infrastructure.* New York: Oxford University Press.

Koonin, Eugene V. 2009. Darwinian evolution in the light of genomics. *Nucleic acids research* 37(4). 1011–1034.

Labov, William. 1986. On the mechanism of linguistic change. In John J. Gumperz & Dell Hymes (eds.), *Directions in sociolinguistics: The ethnography of communication*, 512–538. London: Basil Blackwell 2nd edn.

Langacker, Ronald W. 1987. *Foundations of cognitive grammar: Volume I, Theoretical prerequisites.* Stanford: Stanford University Press.

Larsen-Freeman, D. & D. Cameron. 2008. *Complexity theory and second language learning.* Oxford: Oxford University Press.

Le Page, R. B. & Andrée Tabouret-Keller. 1985. *Acts of identity: Creole-based approaches to language and ethnicity.* Cambridge: Cambridge University Press.

Leach, Edmund. 1964. *Political systems of highland Burma.* London: The Athlone Press.

Lee, Penny. 1996. *The Whorf theory complex: a critical reconstruction.* Amsterdam: John Benjamins.

Lemke, J. L. 2000. Across the scales of time: Artifacts, activities, and meanings in ecosocial systems. *Mind, Culture, and Activity* 7(4). 273–290.

Lemke, Jay L. 2002. Language development and identity: Multiple timescales in the social ecology of learning. In Claire Kramsch (ed.), *Language Acquisition and Language Socialization: Ecological Perspectives*, 68–87. New York: Continuum Press.

Leont'ev, A. 1981. *Problems of the development of mind.* Moscow (Russian original 1947): Progress Press.

Levelt, Willem J. M. 1989. *Speaking: from intention to articulation.* Cambridge, MA: MIT Press.

Levinson, Stephen C. 1983. *Pragmatics.* Cambridge: Cambridge University Press.

Levinson, Stephen C. 2014. Language evolution. In N. J. Enfield, Paul Kockelman & Jack Sidnell (eds.), *The Cambridge handbook of linguistic anthropology*, 309–324. Cambridge: Cambridge University Press.

Lorenz, Konrad Z. 1958. The evolution of behavior. *Scientific American* 6(199). 67–78.

Luce, R. D. 1950. Connectivity and generalized cliques in sociometric group structure. *Psychometrika* 15. 169–190.

Lucy, John. 1992. *Language diversity and thought: a reformulation of the linguistic relativity hypothesis.* Cambridge: Cambridge University Press.

MacNeilage, Peter F. 1998. The frame/content theory of evolution of speech production. *Behavioral and Brain Sciences* 21(4). 499–511.

MacWhinney, B. 2005. The emergence of linguistic form in time. *Connection Science* 17(3-4). 191–211.

Malinowski, Bronislaw. 1922. *Argonauts of the Western Pacific: An account of native enterprise and adventure in the archipelagoes of Melanesian New Guinea.* London: Routledge.

Manning, Patrick. 2005. *Migration in world history.* New York: Routledge.

Marx, Karl & Friedrich Engels. 1947. *The German ideology.* New York: International Publishers.

Mayr, Ernst. 1970. *Populations, species, and evolution.* Cambridge MA: Belknap Press.

Mayr, Ernst. 1982. *The growth of biological thought: Diversity, evolution, and inheritance.* Cambridge MA: Belknap Press.

McConvell, Patrick. 1985. The origin of subsections in Northern Australia. *Oceania* 56(1). 1–33.

Meillet, Antoine. 1926. *Linguistique historique et linguistique générale.* Paris: Champion.

Mesoudi, Alex, Andrew Whiten & Kevin N. Laland. 2006. Towards a unified science of cultural evolution. *Behavioral and Brain Sciences* 29. 329–383.

Milardo, R. 1988. Families and social networks: an overview of theory and methodology. In R. Milardo (ed.), *Families and social networks*, 13–47. Newbury Park: Sage.

Miller, George A. 1951. *Language and communication.* New York: McGraw-Hill.

Milroy, Leslie. 1980. *Language and social networks.* Oxford: Basil Blackwell.

Milroy, Leslie & Wei Li. 1995. A social network approach to code-switching. In Leslie Milroy & Pieter Muysken (eds.), *One speaker, two languages*, 136–157. Cambridge: Cambridge University Press.

Mufwene, Salikoko S. 2001. *The ecology of language evolution.* Cambridge: Cambridge University Press.

Müller, Max. 1870. Darwinism tested by the science of language. *Nature* 1(10). 256–259.

Newell, Allen. 1990. *Unified theories of cognition.* Cambridge, MA: Harvard University Press.

Newman, M. 2005. Power laws, Pareto distributions and Zipf's law. *Contemporary Physics* 46. 323–351. doi:10.1080/00107510500052444.

Norman, Donald A. 1988. *The design of everyday things.* New York: Basic Books.
Norman, Donald A. 1991. Cognitive artifacts. In John M. Carroll (ed.), *Designing interaction: Psychology at the human-computer interface*, 17–38. Cambridge: Cambridge University Press.
Pagel, Mark, Quentin D. Atkinson & Andrew Meade. 2007. Frequency of word-use predicts rates of lexical evolution throughout Indo-European history. *Nature* 449. 717–720.
Parry, J. & Maurice Bloch (eds.). 1989. *Money and the morality of exchange.* Cambridge: Cambridge University Press.
Rączaszek-Leonardi, J. 2010. Multiple time-scales of language dynamics: An example from psycholinguistics. *Ecological Psychology* 22(4). 269–285.
Radcliffe-Brown, A. R. 1922. *The Andaman Islanders: A study in social anthropology.* Cambridge: Cambridge University Press.
Radcliffe-Brown, A. R. 1931. *The social organization of Australian tribes.* Melbourne: MacMillan.
Reesink, Ger, Ruth Singer & Michael Dunn. 2009. Explaining the linguistic diversity of Sahul using population models. *PLoS Biology* 7(11). 1–9.
Ridley, Mark. 1997. *Evolution.* Oxford: Oxford University Press.
Ridley, Mark. 2004. *Evolution.* Hoboken: Wiley.
Rogers, Everett M. 2003. *Diffusion of innovations.* New York: The Free Press 5th edn.
Ross, Malcolm. 1997. Social networks and kinds of speech-community event. In Roger Blench & Matthew Spriggs (eds.), *Archaeology and language I: Theoretical and methodological orientations*, London: Routledge.
Runciman, W. G. 2009. *The theory of cultural and social selection.* Cambridge: Cambridge University Press.
Sacks, Harvey, Emanuel A. Schegloff & Gail Jefferson. 1974. A simplest systematics for the organization of turn-taking for conversation. *Language* 50(4). 696–735.
Sahlins, Marshall. 1999. What is anthropological enlightenment? Some lessons of the Twentieth Century. *Annual Review of Anthropology* 28(1). i–xxiii.
Sapir, Edward. 1921. *Language: An introduction to the study of speech.* Orlando: Harcourt Brace Jovanovich.
Saussure, Ferdinand de. 1916. *Cours de linguistique générale.* Paris: Payot.
Schegloff, Emanuel A. 1968. Sequencing in conversational openings. *American anthropologist* 70(6). 1075–1095.
Schegloff, Emanuel A. 2007. *Sequence organization in interaction: a primer in conversation analysis, volume 1.* Cambridge: Cambridge University Press.

Schegloff, Emanuel A., Gail Jefferson & Harvey Sacks. 1977. The preference for self-correction in the organization of repair in conversation. *Language* 53(2). 361–382.

Schelling, Thomas C. 1978. *Micromotives and macrobehaviour.* New York: W. W. Norton.

Schutz, Alfred. 1970. *On phenomenology and social relations.* Chicago: University of Chicago Press.

Searle, John R. 1983. *Intentionality: An essay in the philosophy of mind.* Cambridge: Cambridge University Press.

Searle, John R. 2010. *Making the social world: The structure of human civilization.* Oxford University Press.

Sidnell, Jack & N. J. Enfield. 2012. Language diversity and social action: A third locus of linguistic relativity. *Current Anthropology* 53. 302–333.

Sidnell, Jack & Tanya Stivers (eds.). 2012. *The handbook of conversation analysis.* Oxford: Wiley-Blackwell.

Simon, Herbert A. 1990. A mechanism for social selection and successful altruism. *Science* 250. 1665–1668.

Slobin, Dan. 1996. From 'thought and language' to 'thinking for speaking'. In J. J. Gumperz & Stephen C. Levinson (eds.), *Rethinking linguistic relativity*, 70–96. Cambridge: Cambridge University Press.

Smith, Adam. 1776. *An inquiry into the nature and causes of the wealth of nations.* London: W. Strahan.

Smith, Kenny, Henry Brighton & Simon Kirby. 2003. Complex systems in language evolution: The cultural emergence of compositional structure. *Advances in Complex Systems* 06(04). 537–558.

Sperber, Dan. 1985. Anthropology and psychology: Towards an epidemiology of representations. *Man* 20. 73–89.

Sperber, Dan. 1996. *Explaining culture: A naturalistic approach.* London: Blackwell.

Sperber, Dan. 2006. Why a deep understanding of cultural evolution is incompatible with shallow psychology. In N. J. Enfield & Stephen C. Levinson (eds.), *Roots of human sociality: culture, cognition, and interaction*, 431–449. Oxford: Berg.

Sperber, Dan & Lawrence A. Hirschfeld. 2004. The cognitive foundations of cultural stability and diversity. *Trends in Cognitive Sciences* 8(1). 40–46.

Sperber, Dan & Dierdre Wilson. 1995. *Relevance: communication and cognition (2nd edition).* Oxford: Blackwell.

Steels, Luc. 1998. Synthesizing the origins of language and meaning using co-evolution, self-organization and level formation. In James R. Hurford, Michael Studdert-Kennedy & Chris Knight (eds.), *Approaches to the evolution of language: Social and cognitive bases*, Cambridge: Cambridge University Press.

Steels, Luc. 2003. Evolving grounded communication for robots. *Trends in Cognitive Sciences* 7. 308–312.

Steffensen, Sune Vork & Alwin Fill. 2014. Ecolinguistics: The state of the art and future horizons. *Language Sciences* 41(A). 6–25.

Stivers, Tanya, Lorenza Mondada & Jakob Steensig (eds.). 2011. *The morality of knowledge in conversation*. Cambridge: Cambridge University Press.

Thomason, Sarah Grey. 2001. *Language contact: an introduction*. Edinburgh: Edinburgh University Press.

Thomason, Sarah Grey & Terrence Kaufman. 1988. *Language contact, creolization, and genetic linguistics*. Berkeley: University of California Press.

Tinbergen, Niko. 1963. On aims and methods in ethology. *Zeitschrift für Tierpsychologie* 20. 410–433.

Tomasello, Michael. 1999. *The cultural origins of human cognition*. Cambridge, MA: Harvard University Press.

Tomasello, Michael. 2003. *Constructing a language: A usage-based theory of language acquisition*. Cambridge, MA: Harvard University Press.

Uryu, Michiko, Sune Vork Steffensen & Claire Kramsch. 2014. The ecology of intercultural interaction: Timescales, temporal ranges and identity dynamics. *Language Sciences* 41. 41–59.

Vygotsky, L. S. 1962. *Thought and language*. Cambridge, MA: MIT Press.

Weinreich, Uriel. 1953. *Languages in contact*. New York: Linguistic Circle of New York.

Weinreich, Uriel, William Labov & Marvin Herzog. 1968. Empirical foundations for a theory of language change. In W. Lehmann (ed.), *Proceedings of the Texas conference on historical linguistics*, 97–195. Austin: University of Texas Press.

Whorf, Benjamin Lee. 1956. *Language, thought, and reality*. Cambridge, MA: MIT Press.

Wierzbicka, Anna. 1988. *The semantics of grammar*. Amsterdam: Benjamins.

Wierzbicka, Anna. 1992. *Semantics, culture, and cognition*. New York: Oxford University Press.

Zipf, G. K. 1949. *Human behaviour and the principle of least effort*. Cambridge, MA: Addison-Wesley Publishing.

Name index

Aikhenvald, Alexandra Y., 46
Atkinson, J. Maxwell, 15
Atkinson, Quentin D., 19
Aureli, F., 16

Baddeley, Alan D., 14
Bakhtin, Mikhail M., 6
Bearder, S. K., 16
Bickel, Balthasar, 44
Bloch, Maurice, 55
Bloomfield, Leonard, 55
Boesch, C., 16
Boto, Luis, 4
Bourdieu, Pierre, 58
Boyd, Robert, 18, 19, 23–26, 32
Brighton, Henry, 11, 19, 23
Brown, Penelope, 14, 51
Bybee, Joan, 19

Call, Josep, 16, 35
Cameron, D., 11, 12
Campbell, Lyle, 22
Chafe, Wallace, 19
Chapman, C. A., 16
Chater, Nick, 19, 23–25
Christiansen, Morten H., 19, 23–25
Clark, Eve V., 14
Clark, Herbert H., 18
Cole, M., 11, 17
Connor, R., 16
Cornish, Hannah, 23
Cowley, S. J., 13

Croft, William, 8, 22, 44, 60
Csibra, Gergely, 14, 32
Curnow, Timothy Jowan, 6
Cutler, Anne, 14

Darwin, Charles, 3, 15, 31, 42, 63
Davidson, Donald, 31
Dawkins, Richard, 3, 4, 15, 21, 37
Di Fiore, A., 16
Dingemanse, Mark, 19
Dixon, R. M. W., 8, 44, 46
Donald, Merlin, 11
Donegan, Jane, 46, 47, 55
Dunbar, Robin I. M., 16, 57, 59
Dunn, Michael, 8
Durkheim, Emile, 39

Eckert, Penelope, 15, 49
Enfield, N. J., vii, 1, 2, 8, 14, 15, 18, 19, 23, 24, 29, 33, 44, 52, 56, 60, 64
Engels, Friedrich, 16
Evans, Nicholas D., 48
Evans-Pritchard, E. E., 50
Everett, Daniel L., 19

Fill, Alwin, 13
Fillmore, Charles J., 44
Firth, Raymond, 50
Fodor, Jerry A., 31
Fortes, Meyer, 50, 51

Gabelentz, Georg von der, 37

Name index

Garfinkel, Harold, 15, 52
Gaskins, Suzanne, 14, 51
Gergely, György, 14, 32
Gibson, James J., 25
Givón, Talmy, 19
Gladwell, Malcolm, 26, 33
Gould, Stephen Jay, 37
Granovetter, Mark, 28
Greenberg, Joseph H., 19
Grice, H. Paul, 15

Hale, Kenneth L., 19
Hare, Brian, 35
Harris, Alice C., 22
Haspelmath, Martin, 44, 56
Hayakawa, Samuel Ichiye, 57
Hedström, Peter, 51
Henzi, S. P., 16
Heritage, John, 15, 52, 53
Hernández-Lloreda, María Victoria, 35
Herrmann, Esther, 35
Herzog, Marvin, 15
Hill, R. A., 59
Hirschfeld, Lawrence A., 58
Hockett, Charles F., 6
Hopper, Paul J., 16
Hudson, R. A., 5, 22, 50
Hurford, James R., 14

Jacob, François, 15
Jefferson, Gail, 15

Kandel, Eric R., 14
Kaufman, Terrence, 6, 56, 58
Keller, Rudi, 22
Kirby, Simon, 11, 19, 23, 60
Klein, Wolfgang, 14
Kockelman, Paul, 15, 30, 33, 39, 43

Koonin, Eugene V., 4
Kramsch, Claire, 11, 12, 17

Labov, William, 15
Laland, Kevin N., 3
Langacker, Ronald W., 44
Larsen-Freeman, D., 11, 12
Le Page, R. B., 5, 33, 50, 55–57
Leach, Edmund, 5
Lee, Penny, 6
Lemke, J. L., 11, 12, 17
Leont'ev, A., 15
Levelt, Willem J. M., 14, 60
Levinson, Stephen C., 14, 52
Li, Wei, 34
Lorenz, Konrad Z., 12
Luce, R. D., 33
Lucy, John, 19

MacNeilage, Peter F., 60
MacWhinney, B., 11, 12, 17
Malinowski, Bronislaw, 50
Malt, Barbara C., 18
Manning, Patrick, 16
Marx, Karl, 16
Mayr, Ernst, 3, 15
McConvell, Patrick, 48
Meade, Andrew, 19
Meillet, Antoine, 37
Mesoudi, Alex, 3
Milardo, R., 34
Miller, George A., 33
Milroy, Leslie, 33, 34
Mufwene, Salikoko S., 63
Müller, Max, 31, 63

Newell, Allen, 12, 17
Newman, M., 17
Norman, Donald A., 30, 33

Name index

Pagel, Mark, 19

Rączaszek-Leonardi, J., 11, 17
Radcliffe-Brown, A. R., 48, 50
Reesink, Ger, 8
Richerson, Peter J., 18, 19, 23–26, 32
Ridley, Mark, 14
Rogers, Everett M., 16, 18, 35, 39, 51, 53
Ross, Malcolm, 21, 33, 34
Runciman, W. G., 16

Sacks, Harvey, 15
Sahlins, Marshall, 49
Sapir, Edward, 19, 30
Saussure, Ferdinand de, 11, 44
Schaffner, C. M., 16
Schegloff, Emanuel A., 15
Schelling, Thomas C., 51, 53
Schutz, Alfred, 15
Searle, John R., 14, 31, 38
Sidnell, Jack, 15, 19
Simon, Herbert A., 14, 32
Singer, Ruth, 8
Slobin, Dan, 19
Smith, Adam, 16, 51
Smith, Kenny, 11, 19, 23
Sperber, Dan, 15, 18, 21–23, 53, 58
Stampe, David, 46, 47, 55
Steels, Luc, 11
Steffensen, Sune Vork, 11–13, 17
Swedberg, Richard, 51

Tabouret-Keller, Andrée, 5, 33, 50, 55–57
Thomason, Sarah Grey, 6, 56, 58
Tinbergen, Niko, 10, 11
Tomasello, Michael, 11, 14, 35, 57
Torreira, Francisco, 19

Traugott, Elizabeth Closs, 16

Uryu, Michiko, 11, 12, 17

Vygotsky, L. S., 11

Weinreich, Uriel, 15, 19
Whiten, Andrew, 3
Whorf, Benjamin Lee, 19
Wierzbicka, Anna, 19, 44
Wilson, Dierdre, 15

Zipf, G. K., 6, 14, 17, 18, 59, 61, 64

Subject index

Aboriginal Australia, 48
actuation, 15
affordances, 25, 29, 30, 32
Alyawarre, 48
antithesis, 42
apes, 35
areal linguistics, 2
Austroasiatic language family, 46
Austronesian language family, 3

Bantu language family, 3
borrowing, 1, 2, 6, 54

case-marking, 44
causal frames, ix, 10, 18, 64
centripetal forces on items, 56
children, 51
cognitive biases, 18, 19
cognitive causal chain, 23
collateral effects, 19
common ground, 6
communication, 2
competence, 8, 57
content-frame fit, 59
contextualization, 44, 54, 55, 60, 61
conversation, 15, 19
cultural totalities, 49, 51, 55
cultural values, 19
culture, 51, 52

Darwin, 7, 24, 63
dependencies in systems, 46

diachronic frame, 11, 15, 16, 18, 19, 21–23, 35, 52, 65
dictionaries, 9
diffusion, ix, 15, 18, 32, 55, 65, 66
diffusionism, 55
diversity, 11
docility, 14, 32
drift, 19
Dutch versus Flemish, 50

emergence, 53
emotion, 40
enchronic frame, 13, 15, 16, 18, 22–24, 35, 52, 55, 56, 65
English, 30, 31, 44
envorganism, 39
epidemiology, 18, 21–23
essentialism, 2
Estonian, 46
ethnographies, 9
evolution, 7, 24
    biological, 3, 4, 9, 14, 35, 63, 65
    historical, 9
    of language, 57
    of language capacity, 14
    of languages, 22
exposure, 27, 28, 65

fashion, 49
feedback, 24
Finnish, 44

Subject index

first language acquisition, 7–9, 14, 21, 24, 56
food chain, as system, 40
form classes, 44
functional association, 40
functional relation, 38

genetics, 3, 4, 7, 37, 47, 56
Geneva Convention, 49
gesture, 15, 33
grammars, 9, 39
grammaticalization, 16, 19
guided variation, 19, 24

historical linguistics, 56
horizontal transmission, 1, 4, 6–8

iambic versus trochaic, 46
identity, 29
idiolects, 6, 55, 63
incorporation, 44, 49, 54, 55, 60
Indo-European language family, 3
inheritance, 1, 2
innovation, 2, 21, 26, 29, 33, 65
internal change, 1, 30, 47*
item-utterance fit, 59
item/system problem, ix, 2, 37, 60, 64
iterated learning, 23, 24
iterated practice, 23, 24, 26

kinship systems, 44, 49, 60

language change, 9, 19, 21, 56, 63, 64
language contact, 1, 19, 47*, 64
language faculty, 25
languages, as unit of analysis, 4, 6, 22, 50, 54, 63
Lao, 44
learning, 30, 32
length-frequency rule, 17, 59

life forms, 3, 4
linguistic item, 5, 39, 54
linguistic items, 6, 22, 24, 60, 63
linkage problem, 17

mainland Southeast Asia, 2
material, 27, 32, 65
memes, 38, 55
metalinguistic stances, 50
micro-macro relation, 51
microgenetic frame, 13, 16, 18, 22–24, 35, 52, 55, 56, 65
minimal effort principle, 17, 18
Mon-Khmer languages, 46
money, 49, 51
MOPEDS framework, 10, 13, 65
motion events, 44
multilingualism, 63
Munda languages, 46

nano-diachrony, 13
natural meaning, 19, 30
normal transmission, 56, 57
normative accountability, 52
normative behavior, 52
Northern Australia, 49

ontogenetic frame, 11, 14, 16, 18, 21, 24, 35, 52, 56, 65
ontology of language, 2, 7, 8, 64, 65
opposite, 42

paradigmatic axis, 45, 58, 61
performance, 8
personality factors, 26, 33
phylogenetic frame, 4, 11, 14, 65
pico-ontogeny, 13
polarity, 46
prepositions, 44

processing, 2, 9, 11
psycholinguistics, 11

relations between relations, 40
representation, 27, 29, 65
reproduction, 3, 27, 30, 52, 65

salience, 29
scales, ix
second language acquisition, 14
sections, 48, 49, 53
selection, 8, 14
semantic change, 21
snowmobiles, 49
social action, 9, 18
social interaction, ix, 15, 24, 32
social networks, 28, 33, 57, 58, 66
sociolinguistics, 31, 33, 66
sociometric closure, 58, 60
sociometric factors, 26
speciation, 3, 4
speech acts, 15
speech community, 6
spoke and wheel, 38
state violence, 52
stickleback fish, 10
subsections, 48, 49
synchronic frame, 11, 16, 18, 56, 65
syntagmatic axis, 45, 58, 61
systems, ix, 30, 37, 39, 40, 50, 54, 56, 58–61, 63, 64

table tennis, 25, 31, 33
Thai versus Lao, 50
time scales, 10–12
trade-off effects, 59
transmission bias
    confirmity bias, 32
    content bias, 30, 31
    context bias, 30, 53
    direct bias, 25, 26, 31
    frequency-dependent bias, 25
    identity bias, 29
    indirect bias, 25, 31, 32
    model bias, 32
    salience bias, 29
transmission biases, 18, 21, 22, 64, 65
transmission criterion, 38, 52
tree diagrams, ix, 3, 7, 8
turn-taking, 15
typologies, 9

universals, 19, 21
utility, 26

variation, 9, 33
vertebrates, 4, 7, 37, 47
vertical transmission, 1, 4, 6, 8

web of inferences, 52
writing, 33

Yupik culture, 49

Subject index